Discovering Stephen Gill

A Collection of Papers and Articles

Discovering Stephen Gill

A Collection of Papers and Articles

Edited by

Nilanshu Kumar Agarwal

AUTHORSPRESS

Worldwide Circulation through Authorspress Global Network
First Published 2008
by
Authorspress
E-35/103, Jawahar Park
Laxmi Nagar, Delhi-110 092
e-mail: authorspress@yahoo.com

Discovering Stephen Gill: A Collection of Papers and Articles
ISBN 978-81-7273-469-5

Printed in India at Tarun Offset, Delhi.

Foreword

When I was approached to write a foreword to the collection of essays on Stephen Gill's literary writings, the first word that flashed past my mind was *Eirenepoios*, the ancient Greek word for 'Peace Makers' or 'Peace Poets'. During the last two decades Stephen has chosen the path of being a torch-bearer for humanity through poetry. His unique poetic prism has shown a powerful array of nuances that shed light for peaceful co-existence. He has shown the power of poetry with its ability to philosophise in his poems as in *Songs of Harmony* and in *Shrine*. His poems have been a vehicle for individual liberation and the discovery of the unknown vignettes in us of the human spirit.

I have known Stephen for almost 35 years. Although a diverse writer of many literary genres, I have known him mainly as a poet transplanted in Canada, who has brought his poetic voice of a South Asian geography and melded comfortably as an illustrious poet with the rest of mainstream Canadian poetic voices. His poetry has bold metaphors of places and the life within these places which shows that he has adapted comfortably to the country in which he lives. Since all Canadians are immigrants, excluding the First Nation peoples and the Inuit, Stephen who has lived in Canada for decades could be classed as a Canadian writer of Canadian literature.

I have watched the mesmeric impact he has had with his audience when I had the opportunity to share the stage with him at readings across Ontario, Canada, and as guest poets at the Austin International Poetry Festival in Texas, in the US. In much of his poetry he has succeeded well in the verbal and structural experimentation of the poetic form. Stephen's poetic hallmark is his rhythmic uncompromising language finding the perfect tongue to make it easy for his readers to understand his celebrations and concerns around him which also happens to be ours. His poetry has been a vehicle for human liberation.

Stephen being a prolific poet and a writer, I congratulate Dr. Nilanshu Kumar Agarwal, the Editor of essays and critiques of his work, as such a collection with the intention of discovering Stephen Gill through the power of his written word is timely to understand this excellent writer and especially through his poetry.

Asoka Weerasinghe
Co-founder of Gloucester Spoken Art,
Poetry & Storytelling Series in Ottawa,
Canada.

Introduction

On the surface, Stephen Gill seems a perfect candidate for postmodern status. A child of Sialkot, his imagination being shaped in the shadows of the snow-covered peaks of Kashmir, he was transplanted to Karol Bagh, New Delhi, where as an adolescent he experienced the horrors unleashed by the partition of India and his family was targeted as Christian. This nightmare led to exile, first to Ethiopia, then to England on the way to a new life in Canada. Memories of this past haunt his writing, ever-present yet at the same time on a long retreat. Cherished foods, clothing and places hold little interest for a people intently watching Hockey Night in Canada on their televisions or navigating standardised streetscapes of doughnut shops and commercial strip malls in their SUV's—though here another snow-covered landscape lies always to the silent north.

In *The Canadian Postmodern*, Linda Hutcheon has identified marginality, or "ex-centrism", as an essential element of postmodernity, noting that Canadians in general perceive themselves as marginalised. Within Canada, she argues, those who are not made to feel part of the dominant culture by reason of race and ethnicity feel even a further degree of marginalisation. Although he has stated his belief that "home is where our feet are," Stephen Gill's position in his adopted land remains "ex-centric". Professor R.K. Singh and Mitali De Sarkar have noted that he "seems to challenge Canadian poets who are skeptical about immigrant poets like him" ("A Search for Elysium", *The Mawaheb International (Canada)*, June 1998), while poems such as "A New Canadian in Toronto", from *Shrine*, in which Gill writes of a city whose lips "smell like plastic flowers," and where "the word friendship/you'll hardly find in its book," speak volumes about his sense of deracination. (He has noted in an interview with Dr. Agarwal, the editor of this collection, that diaspora in Hebrew means exile.)

Stephen Gill's novel *Immigrant* provides further evidence of this sense of alienation. The protagonist, Reghu Nath, a doctoral student at the University of Ottawa, where Gill himself enrolled at the same level of study, finds himself a stranger in a strange land of coldness (both climatic and interpersonal), prejudice and provincialism. Certainly Canada of the 1960s, the historical setting of the novel, though forever congratulating itself on its cosmopolitanism and general atmosphere of tolerance, remained in many ways a bastion of Eurocentric privilege—especially in the publishing and academic worlds, where power was still concentrated in the hands of a WASP elite, primarily in Toronto. Having metamorphosed from a colony of England to what Canadian nationalists argued was a cultural and economic colony of the United States, Canada experienced a schizophrenic geopolitical sense of marginality that must have been a perfect breeding ground for Stephen Gill's personal feelings of diasporic estrangement.

Arriving in Canada in the late 1960s, an exile from the United States during the war in Vietnam, I experienced similar feelings. One of my graduate classes at the University of Toronto was conducted by the then-Master of Massey College in his private living quarters where, in an elegant room furnished with a grand piano and Turkish carpet, we sat at green felt-top tables under eighteenth century prints. In our final class, we were served lunch, with sherry, by the staff, all visible minorities dressed in livery. On this occasion the class was joined by the Master's wife, who discussed with a fellow graduate student, an Englishwoman whose husband was Canadian vice-president of a multinational corporation, their mutual friends in Rosedale and Forest Hill. One of their bridge partners was presently on safari in South Africa: "wasn't that *just* like her?" I was white, of Anglo-Saxon extraction and Protestant upbringing. Even after fifteen years as a foreigner in South Korea and Japan, I have difficulty imagining the degree of alienation that Stephen Gill, with several more degrees of separation than myself, must have felt during his early days in Canada.

Nevertheless, Dr. Gill has always been quick to acknowledge his debt to—and admiration for—Canada and its pluralistic, democratic society. Yet his writing often attests to his personal sense of displacement as a foreigner in a land of foreigners. Professor Singh and Mitali De Sarkar have observed, "Reading Gill's verses one finds he is his Indian self seeking a voice in a new land. His social norms, standards and values are neither fully Indian nor fully Western, but rather international. . . . With the blurring of boundaries in the mental landscape that once surrounded his entire being, Gill is subjected to a nomadic subjectivity concerning his status in a new land. In this new setting he is constantly territorialised, deterritorialised, and reterritorialised . . . ." Again, Stephen Gill seems a perfect embodiment of the postmodern condition.

However, where Stephen Gill decidedly parts company with the postmoderns, with their emphasis upon particularities and, in Linda Hutcheon's words, "acknowledgment of self-situating limitations of address," is in his pursuit, as a humanist, of the universal. (One might note here that Hutcheon has also observed of postmodern fiction that it "is not really any more democratic or accessible than earlier modernist fiction," being equally contrived, manipulative and elitist.) If, as she argues, the postmodern exhibits an "urge to trouble, to question, to make problematic and provisional [the modernist] desire for order or truth," Stephen Gill's work, while acknowledging enormous obstacles to the quest for order and truth, nevertheless insists upon the absolute of universal peace.

Stephen Gill's belief in universality is the cornerstone of his devotion to World Federalism. Rochelle L. Holt has noted that while most writers in the 1990s were struggling to stress the differences between many cultures, Stephen Gill was "professing the opposite, a more complex cognition which the masses have not yet learned in yearning for separate glorification of each race, each colour, each sex, each age . . . the poet tells us through his work that we are beyond brotherhood and sisterhood as we achieve the forgotten meaning of 'neighbourhood', not isolated and separate but one large melting pot where we all appreciate our uniqueness while affirming our similarities" (*The Pilot*, January 20, 1992). In his own words, Stephen Gill, as a citizen of the world, told Professor Jaydeep Sarangi in an interview published in the *Pakistan Christian Post*, "My fellowship with people of diverse creeds has convinced me that people are people. This conviction is based on my visit[s] to different countries. I have discovered that people are people no matter what their beliefs and cultural values are. Underneath their skins they are the same—their hearts and thinking are the same. People everywhere have the same fears, the same hopes and the same instincts for survival."

In an insightful essay that appears within this collection, Shweta Saxena has further pinpointed what essentially divides Stephen Gill from the postmoderns. In her essay, Saxena observes that the images of loneliness and despair that recur in the poems of *Shrine* remind one of Kierkegaard's existential angst. If, rather than dismissing or suppressing such feelings, one 'faces up" to this angst, the possibility for transformation exists. Stephen Gill's poetry and prose never make light of, or avoid, his personal despair; indeed, it might be argued that the overall mood of much of his early verse is one of pessimism and despondency brought on by the stupidity of the human race. However, Gill draws a Kirkegaardian line in the sand, refusing to surrender to his despair. Whereas the postmodern sensibility frequently responds to this condition through the employment of irony and parody, with a concomitant rejection of universals and "master narratives", Stephen Gill expresses what Saxena describes as "full faith in the notion of universal brotherhood." It is this commitment to the absolutes of unconditional love and universal peace that keeps him from retreating into irony, cynicism and relativism.

Where, however, Gill is in accord with the postmoderns is in the desire to frustrate any resolution of differences that involves the absorption of the marginal by the centre, *unless*, for Gill, that centre be one of universal brotherhood where *all* differences are accepted and recognised. Gill's poems do in fact have other characteristics that connect to the postmodern—Patricia Prime has written of his "gift of language, the immediacy of his wit and word-play." However, Stephen Gill's irony is essentially verbal and not deconstructive, nor is it designed to neutralise the possibility of universal truths.

Where, then, does the power of Stephen Gill's verse lie? I recently read an article in a Japanese newspaper about the Free Hugs Campaign, a phenomenon that began in 2001 when an American, whose mother had died, decided to walk Miami Beach holding a sign reading "Free Hugs". The subsequent offer of free hugs by an Australian in 2004 sparked a worldwide movement. A Stephen Gill poem might be likened to a "free hug", not a sloppy or gratuitous gesture but the embrace of a fellow survivor following a cataclysm—along the lines of D. H. Lawrence's "Look We Have Come Through". Stephen Gill survived and transcended the atrocities that he witnessed in his teens through personal and literary acts of courage, drawing a line in the sand that refused despair. In his autobiographical account of this time, he has written:

> It was a shock when I realized that the darkness I left behind had been chasing me continuously. The thought of cruelty of humans always remained in my mind like my own shadow. The more I thought of it, the more I became obsessed to write about it.

Stephen Gill has been able to come to grips with his own-and our collective-anxieties by venturing into the liminal territory of his extremely fertile imagination.

Rochelle Holt has further suggested that there are two types of poets, the "esoteric-academic who yearn for awards, grants and publications by university/commercial presses vs. the poets of the masses who write for the sheer joy of the personally/universally-healing process." Stephen Gill clearly belongs to the latter category. The key to what constitutes the healing process in his work can be found in the love that pervades his art. It is what the American poet and editor Cid Corman would have called the *intelligence* of love. Corman wrote, "it is love that keeps us alive and keeps the works of love alive. Only to the extent that that love is openly and utterly entered into the work has it the capacity to evoke as much. Not IN return, but AS return."

I think it would be fundamentally wrong to regard Stephen Gill's literary quest for world peace as in any way the dream of a romantic—his vision is that of a realist who has witnessed first-hand the unbearable alternatives to universal brotherhood. One is here reminded of George Bernard Shaw's observation that it is the dreamers, not the realists, who believe that the world can continue on its current path without ending in destruction. Whether his subjects be specific, as in the poems "Amputee" and "Mother of an AIDS-Ridden Son", or more general, as in his many peace poems that employ imagery of the dove, Stephen Gill helps us understand that without love and compassion, our lives are essentially meaningless. His splendid haiku, which he calls trilliums, demonstrate his innate sense of love and reverence for all that is life, no matter how commonplace or insignificant the object(s) of his observation might be.

Stephen Gill has been internationally acclaimed for his contribution to global peace. He has been awarded three honorary doctorates, including Honour of Doctorate in Literature from World University in the United States and Doctorate in Literature from the World Academy of Arts and Culture in China. His many honours include Laureate Man of Letters from the United Poets Laureate International, the Pegasus International Poetry for Peace Award, the Global NRI Award from the India-European Union Friendship Society, and The Queen's Golden Jubilee Medal. Poet Laureate of Ansted University, Dr. Gill has been appointed Dean of Creative Writing and Peace Studies at Marquess College in London.

In this age of postmodernity, one senses a growing tendency, especially among the young, who represent our future, to regard life itself as a tired practical joke. Irony has become their front line of defense against dehumanising technology and brutal irrationality, a means of reconciliation to a frightening world where the postmodern appears to be in danger of slipping into the "posthuman". In these dark times of suicide bombers and holy wars, Yeats's rough beast slouching ever closer to Bethlehem, Stephen Gill's work stands as powerful testimony to the nobility and humanity that have always been found in man, yet are much less often found in men. May this bock be a celebration of the life-giving, peace-loving values of a writer who is not merely a national-but properly a world-treasure.

Daniel Bratton
Kyoto, Japan.

Preface

Contemporary world ethos is marked by macabre dance of venomous hatred and ignoble strife. Peace is in peril and human dignity is in disaster. The adders of racial antagonism are ready to devour us. The evils of envy, jealousy, anger and impure desire are distancing us from the emotions of love and sympathy. Religious fanaticism, class-struggles, caste consciousness and racial prejudices have made this world a sterile wasteland, where 'the time is out of joint'. Due to this presence of barren social system, Coleridge's observation 'Water, water everywhere/Nor any drop to drink' seems very relevant.

In such a torpid and sombre world, the creative works of Stephen Gill provide a ray of hope. Through his works, Gill has been able to spread 'rays of peace' over 'the selfish sea of politics'. His message of peace can eliminate 'the withered leaves of greed' and 'the valley of terror' from the world. This harbinger of peace is having several doves (emblem of peace in his poetry) in his hands.

This man of versatile literary genius was born in Sialkot, Pakistan, where he passed his early childhood. He grew in India, where he experienced the fury of senseless religious intolerance. His harrowing experiences in India during the partition days have resulted in the flowering of poetry in him. Those partition period memories of 'stinking atmosphere' haunt Gill even today. He has himself said, "I carry the luggage of my discomforting experiences wherever I go." After his chaotic stay in India, he taught in Ethiopia for three years. After this, he migrated to England and then this creative genius finally settled in Canada. Thus, Gill has experienced diverse cultures. Due to his involvement with various cultures, civilisations and nationalities, he has become a renowned advocate of religious tolerance and multi-cultural coexistence. Through his works, he exhorts the people of the world to shun the reptiles of ethnocentric and jingoistic prejudices, racial antagonism and religious obscurantism.

The present critical anthology is an attempt to examine the various literary merits of this harbinger of peace. The contributors have endeavoured to analyse Gill objectively and judiciously in this critical anthology. I thank all the contributors warmly for their unbiased and penetrating evaluation of Gill's creative works.

I must also express my sense of gratitude to Stephen Gill for sending me his works. I shall ever remain indebted to him for his co-operation and guidance in the completion of this project. Besides, he also posted some of the articles of this anthology on his online Gazette. I thank him for that too.

I am also thankful to Prof. A. N. Dwivedi, with whom I had discussed the whole project and who read its first draft. I must not forget to thank Asoka Weerasinghe and Prof. Daniel Bratton for writing respectively the Foreword and Introduction of the book.

In this academic venture, the role of my wife Shikha is no less important. Without the psychological support provided by her, this literary pursuit might not have been possible. I must thank her for this. My brother Karunesh assisted me in tackling some computer-related problems. I am also thankful to him.

Perhaps, the greatest contribution in the creation of this book is that of Information Technology. Internet has made the world a global village. This wonder of contemporary civilisation made the work of communication easy for me. Almost daily, I had email discussions with Gill about this book and other literary activities. I salute these IT- based Internet services.

Finally, I am thankful to Authorspress for publishing this book.

Nilanshu Kumar Agarwal.

Acknowledgements

The Editor is thankful to the following publications in which some chapters of this book have previously appeared:

a) Asian Tribune online
b) Authors Den online
c) Bridge-in-Making
d) Chowk online
e) Hyphen
f) Pakistan Christian Post online
g) Sulekha online
h) Thanal online
i) The Stephen Gill Gazette online

The Editor is also grateful to Stephen Gill for his encouragement and support in the completion of this book.

List of Contributors

Asoka Weerasinghe is the author of 15 books of poetry. His next work *The Land of Serendipity* is due to be published shortly. His poetry has been published in literary magazines and anthologies in England, Wales, Sri Lanka, US, Sweden, Germany and Canada. He has won the Welsh University Eisteddfod Poetry Award, Sri Lanka State Literary Award, Government of Newfoundland and Labrador Arts and Letters Gold medal for Poetry, Manifold Poetry Award (UK), the Gloucester Arts Board's Arts Award 2000 (Canada), and The City of Ottawa Appreciation Award for Arts & Culture for his poetry. His long poem *Trail of Mankind* was adapted as the storyline for Canada's National Museum of Man's Orientation Hall in Ottawa. He was the guest poet at the Austin International Poetry Festival, Texas, US, in 2001, and also the Co-Founder of the Gloucester Spoken Art, Poetry & Storytelling Series which enjoyed a run of 12 years.

Daniel Bratton is Professor of English in the Faculty of Letters at Doshisha University in Kyoto, Japan. He received his Ph.D. from the University of Toronto, where he taught American and Canadian literature before moving to the Far East in 1994.

A.N. Dwivedi was Professor of English at the University of Allahabad, Allahabad. Currently, he is Professor & Chairman, Department of English, Faculty of Education, Taiz University, Turba, Republic of Yemen. He was conferred the Ph.D. degree in 1975 for his dissertation *Indian Thought and Tradition in T.S. Eliot's Poetry*, which was later published in both India and Austria with a Foreword by Professor Grover Smith of the Duke University, U.S.A. Dr. Dwivedi has published about a dozen books and 75 research papers and serious articles. His papers and articles have appeared in such prestigious journals and periodicals as *WLWE* (U.S.A.), *Explicator* (U.S.A.), *JSAL* (U.S.A.), *WLT* (U.S.A.), *Reviews Journal* (Australia), *The Aryan Path*, *Indian Literature*,

The Banasthali Patrika, *Indian Journal of American Studies* and *New Literary Horizons*. His translations of Hindi poetry have appeared in *Voices of Emergency*, edited by Professor John O. Perry, 1982, and in *The Poetry of R.L.Khandelwal 'Tarun'*, 1991. He has also authored poetry collections, including *Random Reflections*, *Fine Frenzy* and *Protest Poems*.

D. Parameswari is Senior Professor and Head, Department of English and Comparative Literature and Foreign Languages of Madurai Kamaraj University, Madurai. She has done two Ph.D.s, one on Literature and Psychology; and the other on English Language Teaching. Three years back she got her D.Litt., which is the highest degree from a university on women's studies. She has visited countries, including Japan, Hong Kong, the U.S.A., Canada (as a Fellow, with the award of Fellowship by Department of Foreign Affairs, Govt. of Canada, twice), U.K. (on an invitation from Cambridge University), to Sana'a, Republic of Yemen, as a Visiting Professor, and to other countries for attending international conferences and for presenting papers, with financial assistance from those countries. She has produced 20 Ph.D.s, authored five books, and presented approximately 60 research papers in national and international seminars.

T. Ravichandran is Associate Professor of English in the Department of Humanities and Social Sciences at the Indian Institute of Technology, Kanpur. He won the Gold Medal Prize for his Ph. D. work on Postmodern American Fiction from the Department of English, Pondicherry University, Pondicherry. He has published 35 research articles in national and international journals and books on Postmodern American Literature, Postcolonial Literature, Indian Writing in English, Effective Communication, Computer Assisted Language Learning, Cultural Studies, Film Studies, Ecocriticism, and Cybercriticism. He has recently published a book on *Postmodern Identity*.

G. Dominic Savio is Reader in English at the American College, Madurai. He is a prolific writer who has to his credit three books and innumerable research articles. He visited Canada in 1998 on a fellowship awarded by the International Council for Canadian Studies under the Faculty Enrichment Programme. His areas of interest include Comparative Literature, Indian Literature, Canadian Literature, Translation Studies and Women's Studies.

S.J. Kala is Senior Lecturer in English at Fatima College, Madurai. She is working on Stephen Gill for her Ph.D. Her areas of interest include Canadian Studies, English Language Studies, Mass Communication and Journalism.

Ashok Kumar is Reader and Head, Department of English, Feroze Gandhi College, Rae Bareli. He got his D.Phil. from the University of Allahabad in 1993. His book, *The Novels of Manohar Malgonkar: A Study,* shows his sharp critical insight in literature.

Roopali is a Guest Lecturer, Department of English, Feroze Gandhi College, Rae Bareli. She is working on Salman Rushdie for her D.Phil. Degree of Allahabad University.

Sailendra Narayan Tripathy is in the Department of English, BJB College, Bhubaneswar, Orissa. He is the Editor of *Poesie India International.* He has authored five books — *I Am Phallic God And Other Poems*, *My Father In Heaven*, *Hole 'N' Soul*, *The Trapped Word* and *Moon 'N' Cuckoo's Nest* (Edited with Stella Browning and Teresinka Pereira). His poems have been translated into Spanish, Italian and Russian languages.

Kanwar Dinesh Singh is Senior Lecturer in English, Government College, Sanjauli, Shimla. He has doctorate in English literature from Himachal Pradesh University. He has published 10 poetry collections in English and two volumes of poems in Hindi. He also edits *Litcrit India,* a journal of creative and critical writing in English, and *Hyphen*—a monthly of contemporary thought and human values.

Nilofar Akhtar is Lecturer in English at Govt. P.G. College, Champawat (Uttarakhand). She has written scholarly papers and articles.

Nikola Dimitrov is the editor-in-chief of the Roma Destiny National Media in Bulgaria, as well as a board member of eBlessings, a Non-Profit Corporation based in the USA. He also owns a Publishing House in Bulgaria. He is an ordained minister of Living Faith Ministry International, based in Tel Aviv, Israel.

O.P. Dwivedi is a Research Scholar, Department of English, University of Allahabad, Allahabad. The topic of his doctoral dissertation is "A Postcolonial Approach to Three Indian English Novels: Markandaya's *The Nowhere Man*, Rushdie's *Midnight's Children* and Roy's The God of Small Things." He has published a few insightful papers.

Shweta Saxena is a Research Scholar in English, Dept. of Humanities and Social Sciences, IIT, Kanpur. The topic of her research is *Postmodernism in Contemporary Indian English Fiction.*

Nilanshu Kumar Agarwal is Senior Lecturer in English at Feroze Gandhi College, Rae Bareli (U.P.). He was awarded D.Phil. Degree by Allahabad University for his doctoral dissertation on T.S. Eliot. His papers, articles, reviews and poems have appeared in journals and magazines, like *The Vedic Path*, *Quest*, *Pegasus*, *IJOWLAC*, *The Journal*, *Promise*, *The Raven Chronicles*, *Yellow Bat Review*, *Bridge-in-Making*, *Hyphen*, *confluence Blue Collar Review*, *South Asian Review*, etc. He is the Editor of the present anthology.

Stephen Gill is the poet Laureate of Ansted University. He has authored more than 20 books, including novels, literary criticism, and collections of poems. His poetry and prose have appeared in more than 500 publications, mostly in Canada, the United States of America and India. Some of his Urdu/Hindi poems have been sung with music by prominent singers of Pakistan and India. He has appeared in several prestigious national and international reference books, including *Immigrants We Read About* by George Bonavia, International Production, Ottawa; *Who's Who In Canadian Literature*, Reference Press, Toronto, Canada; *Vesta's Who's Who of North American Poets*, Vesta, Canada; *Ethnic & Native Canadian Literature: A Bibliography* by John Miska, University of Toronto Press, *Something About The Author*, Vol. 63, Gale Research, USA; *Who's Who In Canada*, Toronto University Press; and *Who's Who in Ontario*, Heritage Press, B.C., Canada. The present critical articles and papers evaluate his creative works.

P. Raja is in the Department of English, Tagore Arts College, Pondicherry. He has authored 21 books in English and seven books in Tamil. One of his books *A Concise History of Pondicherry* is still in the bestseller list. He is presently working on a five-volume *Encyclopaedia of Pondicherry.*

Ann Iverson is Senior Academic Director of Arts and Sciences at Dunwoody College of Technology in Minneapolis. She has authored poetic collections, including *Come Now To The Window* and *Definite Space*. Her poems have appeared in prestigious publications such as *The Oklahoma Review*, *Margie: American Journal of Poetry*, *Poetry East*, *Water-Stone Review*, *Conte*, *Tarwolf Review*, *Kritya* and others.

John Paul Loucky is Associate Professor, Seinan JoGakuin University, Kitakyushu, Japan. He has taught all areas of TESOL/EFL in Japan for over 20 years. His dissertation compared CALL-based vocabulary learning with Audio-Lingual and Sustained Silent Reading methods. His Homepage at www.CALL4All.us provides a clearinghouse of CALL organisations and a Virtual Encyclopaedia of language education sites for 120 major world languages.

Aju Mukhopadhyay, a bilingual writer, has written poetry, fiction and criticism. He has 12 books in Bangla and 11 in English. His works have been recognised with awards by such bodies as the Writers Bureau of Manchester, American Biographical Institute, Poets International of Bangalore, International Library of Poetry and some others.

Tholana Ashok Chakravarthy is a poet and reviewer, whose poems have been translated into Greek, Spanish, Telugu, Romanian, Chinese, Mangolian, Korean, Taiwanese and Japanese languages. Four volumes of his poetry, titled –*Charismata Of Poesie*, *Chariot of Musings*, *Serene Thoughts* & *Twinkles*—are published till date. He was conferred with Doctor of Literature (D.Litt) by the World Academy of Arts & Culture (UNESCO) and honoured as Universal Peace Ambassador by the Universal Peace Embassy.

Contents

1
"Fissures and Fractures": Identity Crisis in Gill's Poetry

—A.N. Dwivedi

Throughout his poetic career, as also in his life, Stephen Gill has struggled immensely and made a hectic search for self-identity. This search becomes all the more poignantly relevant in view of his relatedness to the country of his birth (India) and the country of his adoption (Canada). He fled from India to breathe an air of freedom in Canada, but in neither land he felt what Milton calls 'peace of mind, all passions spent'. And his discomfort and disquietitude stemmed from the "fissures and fractures"[1] he had experienced in life, specially from the identity-crisis he had suffered in both India and Canada. He himself has described his acute sense of 'suffocation' in his homeland and his harrowing experiences in Canada. In his Preface to *Songs Before Shrine* (2007), which is the focal point in this paper, he writes thus: "I began to flutter my wings to escape the prison of suffocation in search of an El Dorado of peace. The question was how and where to find that El Dorado."[2] This statement of Gill amply shows his predicament at home and in society where he was treated with fear and distrust. His being a Christian aggravated the situation towards the worse. He was insecure everywhere, and nobody cared for his safety and that of his family. Hindus, Muslims and Sikhs were disinclined towards him. He felt, in Chaucer's words, like 'a fish out of pond' in India. The severe identity-crisis at home compelled him to leave for Ethiopia on a teaching assignment, and after three years he went to England and thence to Canada. He has been living in Canada as an immigrant for the last three decades, but there too he is faced with numerous problems, the cultural conflict and the identity-crisis being the worst ones. Through Reghu Nath, the protagonist of *Immigrant* (1982), Gill expresses his bitter experiences of Canada: "Canada had a handful of openings, usually filled by persons born here or by British and American immigrants, who encountered no prejudice because they were not a visible minority like the Africans and the Asians who spoke differently and looked differently."[3] Because of Canada's discriminatory policy, scholars and Ph.D. holders also suffer immensely there, like the Indian Prabha, a graduate in Library Science doing the job of a lowly paid cataloguer, and the Bangladeshi Dr.Hafeez, a renowned scientist in liquid fuel combustion. Several Ph.Ds end up there "rusting, first stinking."[4]

Stephen Gill happens to be a poet, novelist and short-story writer of the Indian diaspora now settled in Canada and doing creative works. As a poet, he has raised his voice against the waves of terror and violence in India and Pakistan during the 1947 partition days, and subsequently he has forcefully pleaded for peace and harmony in the war-torn world of today. In one of his poems, contained in *Songs Before Shrine*, he writes thus:

> For the culture of dialogue
> harmony weaves fabrics
> for warmth
> to womb the fetus of wisdom.
> Harmony
> the author of prosperities
> composes a sonata
> for the piano of delight.[5]

Gill strongly feels that there is a vast cultural gap between the East and the West, and that this cultural gap can be bridged by establishing harmony between them. When harmony is established, a new world order will be created. In this world order, people will live with love and warmth, prosperity and delight. Poems like this one abound in *Songs Before Shrine*, and "Harmony and Peace", "Evening of Harmony", "Rays of Harmony", "When" and some others are the poems of this nature. Bracketed with harmony is the poet's repeated cry for peace in the human world. In reality, harmony and peace have been the burden of his songs in this volume. Realising the great need of peace in the present-day tense world around, the poet utters aloud as under:

> Wearing
> a jacket of peace
> let me swim to the shores
> where freedoms flow.
> I would like to bathe in the waters
> that spout from the fountain
> of your comforting grace.
> ("Peace", *Songs Before Shrine*, p.10.)

No doubt, Gill is a great messenger, even a propagandist at times, of peace, which he often associates with such qualities as love and glory, comforts and prosperity, truth and beauty, delight and benediction. In the poem "My Name is Peace", he says: "I am eternal/ I am peace" (p.11). On the same subject, he writes thus:

> Poetry is to present my vision and my concerns, and to conceive peace in a peaceful way. The compelling influence for my crusade is the peace that is beauty; the peace that is creative; the peace that makes life meaningful. I attempt to illustrate that peace in its myriad forms on the rocks of my words. These rocks shout that Lazarus buried under them longs for life.[6]

Gill has laid so much emphasis on peace and harmony in order to erase the sense of insecurity and tension prevailing in the human world today, and to create such a world-order in which the distracting question of dual identity or multiple identities does not arise. Then only the roaming individuals will be free from the worries of identity crisis.

The identity crisis is usually caused by the overwhelming sense of frustration and alienation. A person travelling to another distant land is bound to undergo this sort of crisis, as in the case of Stephen Gill. Such a person is a victim of displacement and dislocation, both physically and psychologically. Living in another country, he feels an exile who is faced with multiple problems of identity and adjustment. Gill's second novel, *Immigrant,* powerfully evokes the picture of a newcomer from India settling in Canada, and this newcomer is Reghu Nath, an aspirant for the Ph.D. programme in the Ottawa University. Not only does the novel depict the hopes and fears of Reghu but it also gives "an insight into the views immigrants hold of white people and *vice versa*."[7] The predicament of a Ph.D. scholar is beautifully brought out in the poem "A Ph.d. Says":

> I never had time
> to know my rights
> or tread
> that path of romance
> painted by poets. (p.88)

The scholar knows nothing about the world around him except the hunt and the pain of his work. He is confined only to his books and studies. In an alien land, he is a restless soul and no one comes to his help.

If *Immigrant* is an indication of the diverse problems faced by a newcomer to Canada, it becomes more or less an autobiographical account of the writer himself. Some of these problems are: an encounter with the rigid and prejudiced professors at the University, the unfamiliar Canadian accent and register of the English language, the confusing grading system, the adamant Canadian officials, and the haunting memories of the motherland. Of these problems, the last mentioned one makes the immigrant/ newcomer long intensely for his/ her native land and he/ she becomes inescapably nostalgic about it. Then, relations and associations, family and friends crowd up his/ her memories. They 'dance upon the inward eye', as Wordsworth would put it, and remind him/ her of the hearth and home. He/ She then feels a sense of the loss of home or a state of homelessness. In such a situation, he/ she realises emptiness and alienation around and fondly recollects his/ her land and people. *Songs Before Shrine* contains some poems which clearly point to this truth. In the poem "Rocks", Gill compares himself to Lazarus in wistful longing The poet writes here as follows:

> The blooms of my lyrics
> shed tears
> in the night of their
> deep disappointments
> over the fruitless longing.
> Do not stop them
> to uncover their veins
> they borrow my chisel.

and further thus:

> They rend their robes of silence
> to say
> Lazarus buried under rocks
> longs for life. (p.44)

The note of 'longing' and disappointment is paramount here, and the poet-Lazarus deeply wishes to come into life. By means of his lyrics, he wants to get back to the vibrant life he has lost. 'Memory and desire' grip him irretrievably, reminding us of the famous opening lines in *The Waste Land* (1922):

> April is the cruellest month, breeding
> Lilacs out of the dead land, mixing
> Memory and desire, stirring
> Dull roots with spring rain.[8]

There is a certain month or season, when the dear and near ones press upon our memory and desire and then we long to meet them. This applies to all creatures—humans, birds and beasts.

Poems like "My Muse" and "At the Wrong Time" also depict the loneliness and emptiness of the poet-persona in a forceful manner. In a sombre mood, he declares in "My Muse" that he has been able to diffuse 'the darkness of autumn nights' with the help of his Muse, whose benign company can keep off 'the toxic insect of emptiness'. Indirectly, the poet-persona suggests here that he would have felt totally empty and deserted without the sweet, soothing company of the Muse. The other poem, "At the Wrong Time", emphatically brings out the poet's sense of loneliness and helplessness in an alien land. This poem is a clear-cut statement of *what* and *how* the poet feels in the land of his choice. It bears out the fact that the poet is still not free from the identity-crisis (which certainly plagued him and his parental family in Pakistan where he was born as well as in India where he grew up and was educated). In a state of restlessness, he writes in this poem as follows:

> A wing-clipped bird
> I desired wildly
> to hear that voice
> from the bushes of stillness
> when I was away
> from the embraces
> of sleep.

and again in the same breath:

> Even walking
> with the winds of loneliness
> in the dale of woes
> where
> hopes break like weeds
> the same voice speaks. (p.47)

The reader must mark the use of such phrases and expressions as 'A wing-clipped bird', 'the bushes of stillness', 'the winds of loneliness', 'the dale of woes' and 'hopes break like weeds', which combinedly allude to the none-too-happy condition of the poet-persona. He is, instead, leading a life of 'stillness' and 'loneliness' in the midst of festivities going on in the vicinity. He must have looked within and then written the above-noted poetic lines. Evidently, he is a tormented soul drifting here and there in search of his true identity, which definitely eluded him in India and which again proves to be a will-o'-the-wisp in Canada. And both the nations are multi-racial and multi-cultural societies. It is unfortunate that a sensitive person like Gill does not find fulfilling them his heart's desire.

For an immigrant to the West, especially to Canada, it is but natural to come across some problems of distracting fashion. What W.F.Westcott remarks of the protagonist of *Immigrant* is also applicable to the writer of *Songs Before Shrine*. The noted critic Westcott observes about the protagonist of this novel thus:

> *Immigrant* does a fine job portraying a new Canadian's plight. The problems, language barriers, cultural discrepancies, and a longing for the mother country can easily be seen in the strife faced by any new person in any new country.[9]

The various problems confronting a new entrant to Canada, as aptly mentioned by Westcott, are: language barriers (including educational prejudices), cultural contradictions and diversities, and nostalgic recollections of the motherland (which has already been dealt with in this paper). Coupled with these problems are those related to social differences, political and official prejudices, ethnic and social discriminations, and unequal treatment in job opportunities. Some of these problems of the immigrants are fairly highlighted in *Songs Before Shrine*. At many places in this volume, the poet vehemently attacks religious bigotry and fanaticism. Those who spread the fire of violence and distrust in society are called 'reptiles' by the poet. They move about freely under 'the skin of fanaticism'. Speaking of them, the poet writes in the following manner:

> In these sunless lands
> birds of intolerance fly freely
> through the clouds of pitiful ignorance.
> The serpents of racism
> form images here in the mist of fancy,
> spreading the toxin of hate
> to feed the ulcers of anarchy.
> From the cups of their wickedness
> reptiles thirstily drink painful longings
> to see corpses of the innocents
> mutilated by the explosives
> from hidden hands.
>
> ("Reptiles", *Songs* ..., p.59).

They indulge in acts of savagery and wickedness because of their 'painful ignorance' of what they are doing. These 'serpents of racism' spread the air of hate, chaos and anarchy among the people, and take delight in managing the killing of innocent ones. Again and again, the poet returns to such perpetrators of hell; they are impelled by "religious mania" (in the poem "Light of Truth", p.78) and "religious malice" (in the poem "Last Years of the Century", p.105).

Apart from the religious bigots, the poet assails the propagators of ethnic and racial prejudices in *Songs Before Shrine*. These 'racial discriminators', as the poet calls them, are the 'icebergs of venom', and they spread the fire of disharmony among the people. Derogatory adjectives are heaped upon them. They are portrayed by the poet as follows:

> Morn-alarming gusts
> adders of the dust
> stinking vultures
> untouchable for cold intense
> rain-starved
> xenophobic
> uncertain, unsafe
> these smiling shylocks
> rest in rusted tombs.
> ("Discriminators", p.68).

These irrational racists forget the fact that the human world has been drastically reduced today in space and time, and that it has become a meeting-ground for all peoples and races. Instead of monochromatic culture and language, it has now drifted towards multiculturalism and multilingualism. In the present-day global set-up, the sane suggestion of the distinguished critic, Homi Bhabha (who wrote the well-known book, *Nations and Narration*. London: Routledge, 1990), can effectively solve the problem of diverse cultures and languages. This critic has put forward the concept of 'hybridism' in matters of culture and language in the global context. This concept allows cultures and languages, other than one's own, to flourish side by side in a spirit of tolerance and understanding.

Stephen Gill also comes out with a suggestion of his own to overcome the problems of cultural diversity, linguistic barriers, socio-political intolerance, religious fanaticism, and ethnic and racial prejudices, and this suggestion entails the evolving of a universalist stance in these various matters. The need of the hour is to live in an atmosphere of mutual love and trust, and when we learn to live in such a congenial atmosphere, much of the tension caused by the extremist forces will cease and the individuals will be able to emerge out of the identity-crisis and the psychological pressure. One can easily gather the poet's message in the following lines:

> My religion
> was not my choice;
> yet I love all creeds.
> I did not choose
> my tongue either;
> yet I respect all breeds.
> Every culture,
> a beauty of the same garden.
> I am also
> your God's child.
> ("I Am Still a Man", p.61).

The poet has touched here the points of clashes and contradictions the world over — religion, tongue (language) and culture. He then delivers the message of universal love and brotherhood in unequivocal terms:

> I am a human
> I love humankind.
> Smile, my friend,
> because
> we are all one. (Ibid., p.61)

The spirit of this meaningful message pervades the poem "My Canada":

> My Canada
> in thy lap
> lie all nations
> humans and beasts

melt into one shape
under thy care
my Canada. (p.20).

The self-same idea is repeated after two stanzas, and the poet seems a contented man:

Thy soul
a serene temple
for every creed
for every breed.
My heart will sing
always for thee
my lips will chant
night and day for thee
O Canada. (p.21)

Here the poet considers Canada to be a country of diverse creeds (religions) and multiple breeds (races). For this reason, as well as for their living together in a spirit of universal brotherhood, love and compassion, the poet is all praise for this country.

But it is felt in Gill's poetry that all the problems related to creed, culture and race are still not solved. Otherwise, why should he give a clarion call to 'build bridges' in the human world? What is the need of it? Why should he talk of greed-ignited blazes, hostile arms, hearts turning into solid rocks, etc. in a poem like "Let Us Build Bridges"? The clear-cut indication in this poem is that humanity must shun the path of violence and bloodshed and thereby build a happier and brighter future for itself. The closing lines of this poem are worth quoting here:

Many minds
admire sages now
peace cannot swim
on the waves of violence
for a happier future
let us build bridges. (p.111).

'Building bridges' augurs well for the future of mankind, but it requires sincere striving of honest minds towards the goal. Until these bridges are built, the holocaust of the Third World War will loom large over our heads and the overall atmosphere of the world will be fraught with fear and distrust. The divide between man and man, nation and nation, culture and culture, language and language, will continue to persist in the human world. Though Gill tries hard to build "bridges with his books"[10], all is not in his hands. The human world is governed and guided today by self-seeking politicians and power-hungry bureaucrats. In such a situation, the citizens of the world are bound to suffer, both physically and mentally. Their sufferings will lead to untold tension and crisis, including the identity-crisis.

To sum up: the humankind is riven today with numerous problems, and some of these problems are related to language barriers, cultural contradictions, ethnic and racial prejudices, religious fanaticism, and socio-political discriminations. Stephen Gill, as a sensitive poet, is fully aware of these disturbing problems leading to insurmountable tension and crisis in human minds. He suggests, with a streak of idealism, that peace and harmony are the thinkable remedies for them. He also suggests that the universalist stance might solve the problems. But as the reins of power lie in the hands of wily politicians, it is somewhat difficult to arrive at a solution of the raging problems of today. Gill knows this fact very well, and hence mental tension and identity-crisis continue to plague him in his poetry.

Notes & References

1. Patricia Prime, "*Shrine*: Poems of Social Concerns", *The Mawaheb International* (June 2000), p. 4.
2. Stephen Gill, "Preface", *Songs Before Shrine* (New Delhi: Authorspress, 2007), p.xi.
3. Stephen Gill, *Immigrant* (Ontario: Vesta Publications Ltd., 1982), p.25.
4. Ibid., p.111.
5. Stephen Gill, "Harmony", *Songs Before Shrine*, p.19. Subsequent references to this text (poems) are given in the paper itself.
6. Stephen Gill, "Preface", *Songs Before Shrine*, p. xxi.
7. D. Parmeswari, "The Cultural Baggage: A Reading of Stephen Gill's *Immigrant*", *Glimpses*, ed. Hamadan Darwesh (Ontario: Vesta Publications Ltd., 2005), p.137.

8. T.S. Eliot, "The Burial of the Dead", ll.1-4, cited from *The Waste Land and Other Poems*, 1940 (London: Faber & Faber, 1972), p.27.
9. W.F.Westcott, "*Immigrant*", *Christian Monitor* (November 1980); cited from D. Parmeswari's article in *Glimpses*, ed. Hamadan Darwesh (2005), p.137.
10. See *Daily Expositor* (Canada) on the flap of *Songs Before Shrine* (2007).

2

The Dialectics of Diasporic Experience: A Reading of Stephen Gill

—D. Parameswari

Diasporic writing, a post-colonial scenario elaborates issues such as marginalisation, cultural insularity, social disparity, racism, ethnicity, etc. These writings address problems that arise from the transnational space created by a fluid community that is neither at home nor outside, that neither gets amalgamated with the new culture nor decides to move back to the origin. Oscillating between the attractions of home and those from the new, the migrants wage a constant psychic battle: the old world is replete with myth and tradition; the new world order is proliferate with thirst for freedom and independence. They are in a dilemma as to whether they should remain in a ghetto of old values with least interaction with the majority, or break the barriers and get assimilated with the overwhelming new culture.

The term 'diaspora' originally related itself to the Jews, their exile and alienation, but today it covers migrations, the transmission of one national tradition to another and globalisation too, at large. The diasporic individual is no more a Jewish victim-type as his transmission is a self-choice and a voluntary option for opportunities of study, growth and employment. In the self-chosen new land, he has to either get integrated with the changed social and cultural set-up, and demarcate a new transnational identity, outwitting his motherland's cultural pulls and value-allurements, or remain in an ivory tower, in absolute isolation.

The 'Politics of Culture' as addressed by Edward Said in his deliberations on 'Orientalism' introduces the theory of migrant sensibility. Cultural politics, as specified by Said, is a component of location/space. Cultural politics becomes the battleground for arguments when the Orient moves towards the Occident, either for a merger, or to create a ghetto. In this stride towards the new land, there is a simultaneous nostalgia as the dear native land has its own rich tradition, attractive landscape and wonderful inhabitants which are to be almost forgotten; he is now obliged to develop a sensibility which can be phrased as compromise, negotiation and assimilation! An Indian migrated to Canada has to look upon himself as a Canadian; if he were in U.S. he is expected to conduct himself as an American. This kind of compromise that involves a necessary self-transformation presupposes pain and frustration to the immigrant. It is a moment of self-effacement that brings him a lot of emotional strain. Though Canada has a very generous political policy when it comes to immigrants, there is no 'melting pot' syndrome everywhere. There are numerous belts of people with distinct ethnic features and identities. The picture is that of 'salad bowl' where the components exist with distinct identities.

The India-born diasporic writer Stephen Gill, well known as the author of several novels, short-story collections, poems and prose writings, is concerned with the dialectics of the immigrants' experience in the Canadian soil. His novel *Immigrant* spins around the plight of the Asians, particularly an Indian who enters Canada, 'the land of his dreams', to pursue higher studies. The protagonist Reghu Nath confronts several situations, pleasant and unpleasant throughout his journey from his motherland to Canada. He approaches the International League Office which allots him a quiet and comfortable room. Evading sleep, tossing in bed he recalls the posters he saw in the Canadian embassies in New Delhi and London, proclaiming Canada as a land of opportunities; he remembers his compatriots who told him that the Indians who go abroad finally settle down only in Canada. He has been further told that people in the U.S. and Canada are honest and hard-working, compared to the Indians. He is confident that if he were nice to his professors he would be well taken. He decides to be polite, meek and honest.

Reghu, subsequently, paints a dream picture of the university where he will be a student. He contends that it will be an ideal place, entirely different from such institutions in India where segregation on grounds of gender and caste is a norm. In India he was never able to express his feelings to any member of the opposite sex. Perhaps, it was his shyness, or male ego which stood in the way. He also feels that people in India do not practise or think of love as a serious matter. Now he is happy that he is free to carry out whatever he has read or heard.

The diasporic individual Reghu is gradually surrounded by a number of problems related to communication. He is not conversant with telephone talks and telephone-talk manners. A woman who answers his call talks in unintelligible English. Dropping into a sofa in despair he visualises his future as bleak and hopeless. He apprehends that he has to thus suffer a communication problem which he has already experienced with some American and English people. He is able to communicate easily with the French, Italians, Germans, Africans and people of other nations. His basic problem is only with certain types of British and the North Americans. He blames the educational system in India which did not introduce him to the accent or the colloquial expressions of the English-speaking countries.

All immigrants, during their stay in the new land, encounter culture-conflicts and shocks; some easily divulge while others require time. A few others do not/ refuse to yield. Reghu's incompatibility with the Western culture surfaces when he reaches the university hall where he notices that everyone except himself is in casual dress; he has come in business suit. He feels uncomfortable as he seems to be the centre of attraction due to his clothes, obviously not tailored in a North American style and also because he is wearing them in such suffocating weather. This embarrassment adds to his depression and desperation. On another occasion, he is terribly shocked when he is told that holding another man's hand can be misunderstood as a gesture of homosexual companionship which is uncommon in his country.

The other culture shock Reghu receives involves the women he meets and their style of living. Queen of Sheba with whom Reghu becomes friendly is a talkative intellectual, a native of Trinidad, in her thirties. She discusses anything on earth with ease and fluency. She suggests to Reghu to move to New York for money and recognition. She comments, Canadians are prejudiced and they suffer from the worst kind of inferiority complex. She relates this to her experience in the States:

> I discovered that people in the States care for talent. They don't see colour or race; they look for the people who can do the job. All the blacks who are holding high positions in Canada, and to some extent also in the States, are far superior in intelligence and talent than the whites with the same qualifications. Believe me, Canadians will never give responsible positions to blacks, easily. (44)

While leaving his room Sheba invites Reghu for supper. In her apartment, while preparing the supper she suggests to Reghu to make use of some of the old women-like Mrs. Wallace, for his benefit. Reghu's culture shock consummates here, the shock unique to this immigrant.

A few other shocks are the order of the day for a diasporic man. As advised by the Black Queen Reghu becomes friendly with Mrs. Wallace, his neighbour, who is understood as a renowned writer. One day he invites her for a drink. He is eager to collect information about Canada's and particularly Montreal's literary scene, about successful Canadian writers, to see if there is a possibility of making a living by writing. However, when he attempts to focus their talk on these areas, the Black Queen moves on to something else. Reghu slowly comes to know that she has never published any book; hers are only journalistic articles in local newspapers. Appearances are deceptive, he understands.

Yet another concern of Gill in *The Immigrant* is with the immigrants' difficulty in securing permanent job in the new soil. Day by day Reghu finds his stay in the university intolerable, an unbearable mental torture for him. Neither the courses nor the grades this foreigner finds suitable. After spending two months, Reghu leaves the university. Hoping to get a job he approaches Canada Man Power Office but feels disappointed.

He runs down the memory lane with regard to his own country where he held a good position before coming to Canada. It would be hard to return to find another job in his country which is beset with problems of its own. Besides, he has lost contact with his friends and acquaintances. He finds himself unable to get a suitable employment in Canada. Securing a satisfying position becomes a Herculean endeavour. He is offered temporary jobs for a few weeks. He sends applications to various offices, universities and colleges but is advised to obtain his citizenship which would enhance his chances of securing a job. He renounces his Indian citizenship for a Canadian one. Yet the situation does not improve any way. Once he realises that his stay in Ottawa for three years does not serve his purpose, he decides to move to Montreal in search of a new way of life.

Reghu has already lived in Montreal once before to take a seminar course at Sir George Williams University. He comes to Ottawa filled with memories of Montreal to gloat over. He has always longed to return to Montreal where nobody takes exception to any creed, class or colour. He finds a great change in these three years. He meets different types of people. One of his neighbours often compliments him on his handsomeness and youth. Reghu is not able to tolerate. Irritated, the neighbour thunders, "You'd better keep out of my way. Why don't you go back to your country?"(42) But Reghu has by now mellowed and with a lot of endurance, he replies, "Where? The whole world is my country. I'm a world citizen" (42). This is a typical attitude which a representative immigrant develops after a long stay.

The diasporic man maps his vision of life in order to transform his attitudes. Reghu slowly develops a tendency to give in though he is angry at being cheated on several occasions. He is sorry that things aren't working out. He is a peace-loving and law-abiding citizen, yet he hates to think there is no freedom to do what he likes as long as he does not disturb others. He is in a mood to drink, in order to shed his tears and inhibitions. He also wishes to dance and dance, till every limb of his body becomes exhausted, and he does so. Feeling sick he vomits on the floor, for he thinks he need not be concerned about others when no one is bothered about him. Perhaps, this is his revenge against the strange new land which oppresses and horrifies him. However, this gloomy stage is only temporary in the immigrant's life, as he soon envisages a bright future in the new, alien soil. Next morning he moves to Montreal, dreaming of 'fresh woods and pastures anew'.

Reghu is always aware that he is from a land of culture and rich heritage. He is from a land where family ties are held sacred, and special regard for parents is a virtue of utmost importance. He is from the country of Rama, a person who willed to spend fourteen years of his youth in a jungle in exile to please his father. Also Reghu is from the nation of Saravana, a man who carried his old, blind parents on two baskets hung on his shoulders and walked across India to satisfy their wishes to visit the holy shrines. Now Reghu can declare to every Canadian that he is a product of that sacred cultural environment. He wants to stay in the mainstream-values of the country in which he was born and where he has left a part of himself. Both Gill and his protagonist glorify their own land which is a land of culture and heritage. He alludes to *Ramayana*, one of the Indian epics, to highlight the fact that parents are worshipped in India, through heroes like Rama and Saravana.

His friend, Mrs. Wallace, introduces Reghu to a woman whose brother's wife is from Ceylon. Mrs. Wallace tells Reghu that her family expects the girl to be obedient, faithful and patient like other girls from the east, and that after the marriage they have discovered that she has none of these qualities. If the family is disappointed in one way, the girl, in another, all originating from varying cultures, differing societies and contrasting perceptions. Mrs. Wallace continues, saying that she compels her husband to work harder and harder to make money in order to buy her more material comforts. Reghu argues,

> "Mind you, all women from the east are not like her."
>
> "I believe you can still find many women in India who respect their husbands more than most western women do."

The immigrant Reghu thus holds that his own people and their culture are adorable, as they cherish emotions like love, affection, and filial ties sacred. He soon meets Maple, a divorcee in her thirties. One day, after the dance, when he asks her something very personal, she replies that they have to know each other first. Reghu does not agree, but Maple persists:

> "A woman has to be emotionally involved with a man before she gives herself to him."
>
> "For me, friendship is one thing, but marriage is another. Marriage is more than a mere friendship between souls."
>
> "Don't you think a common background, outlook and dates are important for a successful marriage?" (24)

At this point Reghu becomes furious and retorts:

> Not at all. I can give you examples of many couples who have nothing to share. Yet their married life is happy. There are still many more who settle down after going together for years under the pretext of knowing each other and whose marriage is on the rocks. I mean intellect is deceptive. (24-25)

The author delineates two different worlds, two cultures, Eastern and Western. Maple represents modern civilisation which appears to have robbed man's emotions and natural impulses while Reghu Nath epitomises the oriental culture of his country. There prevails a tendency towards compromise, adaptability and compromise in the east, whereas the west seems to subsist on incompatibility, separation and divorce. Recalling an incident he came across while travelling back to Cornwall by train, he comments that though Canada is a democratic country, its citizens are living in a police state. Mrs. Wallace and Reghu are often critical of Canadian police and its system of law and order.

Dialectics of Reghu's diasporic experience is apparent. He is not a fanatic as he does not passionately cling to his native tradition and culture. He evinces a generous tendency to appreciate the global culture, at significant moments. At Montreal he is beset by several situations where his mind draws comparisons between the culture of his origin with that of the new. In one such, his Indian friend Mohan asserts, "a girl in

India would accept an invitation [from a male] only after a good amount of thinking. That is why such meetings in India often end in a marriage. In Canada, the situation is different. If a girl accepts tea or any other kind of drink, it does not mean that she concedes to be your girl friend" (65). Mohan adds that Indian girls still respect their husbands. Reghu reacts saying that men and women all over the world are the same basically and these so-called cultures are man-made and meant to cause only confusion and anarchy. He reasons out:

> Look, the world is changing fast everywhere. A university- bred girl from India can be a worse wife than a Canadian-educated girl. Women are seeking liberation even in India. (66)

This is one instance of Reghu's tendency to adjust himself to the new land, his ability to comprehend the cultural oasis which is the essential requirement for a diasporic individual.

An immigrant runs into a good lot of fellow immigrants who are victims of discrimination in one way or the other. He finds them lifeless, dead bodies. At Ottawa later, Reghu is given to know the tragic predicament of several misplaced Indians in Canada. He understands that a student was permitted to pursue his doctorate in English Literature though he had his masters degree only in Hindi. Reghu is next pained to hear that Prabha, his Indian friend, committed suicide by jumping from a tower of the parliament building. The following day he reads an account of Prabha's death in a local newspaper which says it is a calculated step; he is not able to sleep the night he learns about this death and the report. He feels lonely, a foreigner in a foreign land. He realises that nothing brings men lasting happiness. He thinks of Tolstoy who continuously sought peace of mind, and often thought of killing himself though he had wealth, good health, and obedient children. He regrets that Prabha's knowledge, her education, her parents' sacrifice, her life and everything ended in nothing. He there are some more moving dead bodies in Canada, without any hope; their ambition killed by the tall, cold towers of indifference or discrimination.

Before him there emerges the picture of a moving dead body, Dr. Hafeez, a scientist from Bangladesh. Dr. Hafeez proposes to serve as

Visiting Professor in Canada and applies for the same with the department of Chemical Engineering, which offers him very little opportunity to do research in combustion. Meanwhile, he is constrained to give up his job and go to Bangladesh to attend his brother's funeral. When he returns after six months, he tries hard to find a position in the area of his interest but is not successful. He begins to face problems of food and rent; he contacts industries and even technical colleges, but receives negative answers. In despair, he leaves Canada for Bangladesh in spite of the fact that he hates and fears the unsettled political climate of his native country.

Reghu's mind then drifts to another dead body who is a Ph.D. in Political Science from India. He accepts a waiter's work in a Toronto restaurant. He likes the work as he is free from preparation for classroom lectures, examinations and evaluation of answer scripts. Money and carefree existence make him contented. The atmosphere, however, deadens his soul. The next person in Reghu's list is from Pakistan, a Ph.D. in Computer Science from a university in France; though he is a bilingual he has no job. He is agonised at the thought that all these Ph.D.s and many others have given almost half of their lives to learning. Their parents have spent money and sacrificed their own comforts in order to give them the best possible education and sent them to Canada with high hopes. But they are rusting and stinking. He is sure that white Canadians take him for a starved Asian, a gold digger, an opportunist, a mystic, a meek, non-pacifist, sex-maniac, a symbol of eastern wisdom and what not. But none attempt to unlock his innermost recesses to unearth his dormant desires.

R.T. Robertson, a Canadian scholar, remarks in an unpublished paper, as cited by C. D. Narasimhaiah, that all New Literatures including the diasporic originate from two historical experiences: from leaving one's own home; and being in a new, sometimes invading culture. The physical and psychic disturbance of wandering between two worlds, physically here and mentally there, creates exceptional situations. In the novel under discussion the immigrant prepares himself psychologically to become the son of this strange, new land. One morning when Reghu is sipping his tea, Mac, a businessman from India comes with his white girlfriend Grace to meet him. He is a cheat; he fools Grace saying that he is from a Maharaja's family. Mac plants in the minds of Grace and Sanjay the idea of running a garment store on a partnership basis. Telling a number of lies he manages to get money and open a shop in Ottawa. Sanjay and Grace leave the shop once they understand that they are deceived by Mac. Mac now tells Reghu that it is possible for him to run a business without money as he did. But Reghu denies and advises:

> But I believe in honesty and hard work. The business which is based on dishonesty cannot go very far. There is a limit beyond which it cannot flourish—it'll either collapse or remain static. To run such a business is like building a house on sand. (146)

Mac continues to insist on the comforts that Reghu would enjoy if he follows his directions. He encourages him to be the manager of the cinema house he is going to purchase soon. Instead of answering, Reghu looks out at the snowflakes falling outside. He notices the table set with chicken curry and chapattis which he has been missing so long. Ultimately, he smiles, the smile implying his willingness to yield to the pull of the new land; he now has assimilated himself to new cultural and spatial environment; this new identity has ironed out his conflicts about values and standards, and has helped him to adapt himself to the new living space.

In a migratory encounter, when a diasporic individual is capable of networking with the people of the new country his new-found sense of solidarity boosts his morale and guides him to anchor himself in the new home. As nothing hinders the onward march of this migrant who good-humouredly loses sight of the protruding edges, he is in the cultural construct of the 'melting pot' where the stranger becomes the native son of the new but comfortable land. The fact that the Ireland-born Joyce lived in Zurich, the Poland-born Conrad lived in England, the Guyana-born Indian-Canadian Cyril Dabydeen settled in Canada and the German translator-cum-author Felix Paul Greve became Frederick Philip Grove in Canada speaks for the immigrant's need to adapt. Reghu's merger with the Canadian culture is symptomatic of his new-found knowledge that "Home is where the feet are, and we had better place our heart where the feet are." His home now has moved from India to Canada, the wheat-granary of the world which generously embraces its prodigal son.

Instead of viewing the diasporic text as the same or the other in the new land, it would be relevant to read them as hybrids of the similar and the dissimilar. A reader need not be inquisitive to locate them in one of these binaries, but learn to reread/reinterpret them as rich and meaningful documents on which is superimposed the entire gamut of a diasporic individual's social and psychological conflicts. Despite the long suffering, a gradual acceptance and a final assimilation manifest themselves in this individual who evinces traces of perseverance, fortitude and spiritual stamina. Bharati Mukherjee once said, "...in the U.S. I am allowed to see myself as an American. It is a self-transformation" (Qtd. in Ketu H. Katrak, 213). It is this kind of change/acceptance/negotiation the diasporic individual develops ultimately. His is a journey that involves the dialectics of revolt and acceptance.

The multiple and diverse order we live amidst today has put us in great problems in this multicultural and globalised world. "The process of globalisation has not only unsettled people and cultures but has created new identities and affiliations in terms of both conflicts and collaborations (Baral & Kar 2003 11). Great art is a unified product; a writer is a unifier. A diasporic writer is a greater unifier; the more the diversity he delineates, the greater are the possibilities for the merger. The dialectics he portrays are paradoxically persistent and resolved too.

Works Cited

Amirthanayakam, Gay. *Asian and Western Writers in Dialogue: New Cultural Identities*. London: Macmillan, 1982.

Baral, K. C. & Kar Prafula, ed. *Identity: Local and Global*. New Delhi: Pencraft international, 2003.

Dabydeen, Cyril. "India in Me: Reflections", *Writers of the Indian Diaspora: Cyril Dabydeen*. Ed. Jameela Begum. New Delhi: Rawat Publications, 2000.

Gill, Stephen. *Immigrant*. Ontario: Vesta, 1982.

Katrak, Ketu H. "South Asian American Literature", *An Inter-Ethnic Companion to Asian American Literature*. Ed. King-Kok Cheung. New York: CUP, 1997.

Parameswaran, Uma. "Home is Where Your Feet are, and May Your Heart be There too", *Writers of Indian Diaspora: Theory and Practice*. Ed. Jasbir Jain. New Delhi: Rawat, 1998.

Singh, R. K. "Cross Cultural Communication", *Language Forum,* Vol. XXIV, No. 1-2, Jan.-Dec. 1998.

3

Green Dove in the Shrine: Ecoconcerns in Stephen Gill's *Shrine*

—*T. Ravichandran*

"A person is largely the product of the environment."

—Stephen Gill, *Shrine* 24

Surfeit of critical materials and review articles on Stephen Gill's poetic oeuvre calibrate the poet behind the poems as an apostle of peace, a harbinger of love and a propagandist of universal harmony. Naturally, Stephen Gill, originating from that part of Punjab merged with Pakistan after 1947, having witnessed in close quarters the atrocities caused during the Partition period in the Indian sub-continent, and sandwiched between Indo-Pak pangs, advocates peace, love, and harmony through his poems. Yet, the excess of criticisms that focus on these overt aspects fail to highlight other subtly significant features of Gill's poems. Particularly, a much-ignored feature that is very much embedded in these aspects is the poet's concern for nature, environment and ecological balance. This paper attempts to illustrate the point that the predominant motif underlying all of Stephen Gill's poems is essentially ecological. As the pacifist aspects of Gill's poems are represented by "white dove", and as this paper studies the ecoconcerns of his poems specially focused on his collection *Shrine*, figuratively, "green dove" is used to address them.

An Ecocritical reading of Gill's poems suggests that there is an underpinning concern for the earth, the environment, and the nature.

Stephen Gill is very much prophetic in this regard. What is striking in *Glimpses* is the passage in which he reveals he is more of a prophet with a mission. He envisages: "In order to achieve something meaningful, particularly in the field of creative arts, including singing, dancing, writing, speaking, one needs some power behind. To attract that power, one should depend on one's own power first. One should not ignore external powers" (81). Gill derives this power by considering him as an integral part of a holistic nature that is responsible for maintaining ecological equilibrium. In the following paragraphs, I would like to render this sense of an internal power backedup by external powers as something emanating from a fine ecological vision.

Stephen Gill's keen awareness of the environment can be noted even in his *Songs Before Shrine*. In the poem, "When I See", the poet sharply points out the disruption between nature and man-made environment. He writes:

> When I see
> the blades of grass growing
> trees leafing
> birds awaking us
> I think of
> the mounting cries. (55)

The poet sees growth as an organic process, whereas, in sharp contrast to natural growth that is progressive, he finds human beings subsumed by woes taking regressive steps. Environmental pollution is the major culprit in his subsequent observation:

> When I see
> people jogging at ease
> heading towards the beach
> searching clean, fresh air
> I think of
> polluting smogged sights. (56)

The elements of nature are in general well integrated and merge with each other effortlessly. But, whenever they come in contact with the disruptive human influence, they too are contaminated. In the poem, "Snowflakes", Gills uses the image of snowflakes to exemplify this notion. The same snowflakes, when likened to a dove, are soft and gentle but when the comparison is extended to human beings, they become hard and slippery. He writes:

As feathers of a dove
soft and silky
snowflakes fall.
With nature's gentle hands
they shroud
the vastness of the evening.
These dews of indifference
descend to the trees
slanted roofs
deserted roads
and windy paths.
As a human heart
they would grow
slippery and hard
when men and beasts
stamp on them. (82)

Functionally, Stephen Gill's ecoconcerns are worked out in his poems at two levels. At the first level, as it is evident from the discussion on "Snowflakes", he makes use of figures of speech, particularly similes and metaphors. At the second level, he makes direct address to nature. In "Wind", for instance, he envies it for its "untamed", "unbound" freedom. None the less, it reveals to him the constricted life of humanity. He admires the wind in the following lines:

You rage
you smile
you hiss
you cry
depending on your moods.
How lucky you are!
Any shape you wish
you assume.
Unlike humans
you are free. (86)

Similarly, Gill's "A Breeze That is Free" also associates liberty with the elements of nature. Yet, the poet wishes to use "breeze" to freshen up the intellectual mind that is suffocated with contaminating thoughts. Hence, he desires to act like a breeze:

> If I were a breeze
> I should lull the learned
> to bar the door of his thinking
> from breeding substances
> that pollute our planet
> and fill him with a treasure
> that is possessed by the fields
> filled with trees. (107)

A replacement of the dry but corrupting intellect with lush ecosphere would lead to sustainable development that can enliven human beings and their surroundings.

In similar vein, the poem, "Enigma", juxtaposes the natural with the synthetic and leaves the choice to mankind. The first stanza begins with an Edenic, idyllic, prelapsarian setting:

> On the one side
> I smell
> the delicious odor of pleasing sights
> of the lakes of fresh water
> plunging spectacular cliffs
> and a field
> with smiling flowers
> and butterflies.

In Peter Barry's description of the "outdoor environment", this picture clearly falls under the classification of "'the scenic sublime' (e.g. forests, lakes, mountains, cliffs, waterfalls)" (255). This scenic sublime is contrasted with a postlapsarian, artificial atmosphere in the following stanza. As Gill mentions,

> On the other
> I see
> an island seduced by technology
> where a kite is trying to fly. (100)

The wantonness of the sportive butterflies is replaced here with a paper kite that struggles to fly. The ecoconcern that human beings should express lies enigmatically "in between" in the form of "a slumbering dove on the steps of a rusting ladder" (100).

Shrine is subtitled as *Poems of Social* Concerns; however, the whole collection can be viewed as "Poems of Ecological Concerns". At the outset, the author recalls his past in his preface where he shudders to remember the partition riots that he witnessed literally from close quarters. The human violence caused in mutual ill will between the Hindus and the Muslims is also perceived as an act against nature. Or, rather, it is nature that forebodes such violent happenings. Gill conjectures: "Every time there was a stir caused by the wind, a car on the street, the bark of a dog, or the mew of a cat, we froze inside our house" (8). Later he observes that the city, New Delhi, smells rotten with the stench of the dead bodies. Nevertheless, he is equally distressed to see that the decomposed bodies pollute the environment too: "Even the water became polluted because several dead bodies were thrown in the Yamuna River which was the source of supply for the city residents" (11). When the Hindus were rescued by the Gorkha soldiers, while moving on their way to India, "they found the wells and tanks filled purposely with the carcasses of animals and other dirty elements to pollute the water." It points toward a loss of ecological balance. Entropy, indicative of dissipation and waste, predominates with the waning of energy. With this prelude, the poet sets appropriate ground for the symbiosis of energy and ecology. Literally as well as figuratively, he describes, "the frustrations of my (his) anguished soul that went in search of an oasis" (23).

Even Gill narrates the whole trauma he underwent in ecological metaphors. During the days of turbulence when he expected that he being a Christian, the Bishop of New Delhi would send a vehicle to rescue him and his family, he is disappointed to note, "how easily shepherds can forget their flock" (13). By this metaphor, he identifies the innocent victims as "sheep". Often he associates unpleasant, fearful, and cruel things with "wolf" (19) and "shark" (25) whereas the fertile things of life, such as the poetic imagination, are referred to in terms of "plants" and "crops" (26). Thus he mentions about fear: "Fear as a wolf of painful emotions kept emerging again and again from the bushes of helplessness in the wasteland of time" (18). In order to escape from the onslaught of the religious fanatics, the innocent people hide "themselves in the crops of sugar cane and cotton" (20). Ultimately, it is nature that gives them asylum.

Nature is seen as a free being living for its own sake and expressing its own desires in an unrestrained, unconditional manner. In

"Me", Gill uses the image of water to represent this: "I want to express my self / drink my own water / flow in my own way / live in me" (31). The poet reiterates this view firmly in the poem, "Who Shall Buy". The qualities of nature such as "the warmth of the valleys", the poet sharply comments, cannot be commodified. He spells out this idea in the following lines:

> No one can buy
> nor sell
> the freedom of the winds
> the grace of the lakes
> the dignity of the palm trees
> the mystery of the oceans
> the sobriety of the jungles
> and the songs of the seasons. (32)

He further points out the symbiotic and homogeneous relationship that exists between nature, man, and the surrounding universe in these lines:

> No one can buy
> nor sell
> the fragrance of the flowers
> which is a friend of the universe;
> and the inter-dependence
> of all animals, nations and nature
> who form a family with humans
> and who breathe
> the same air
> under the same canopy. (32-33)

"Image of Flowers" is a very interesting poem from *Shrine* as it is brings out centrally Gill's ecoconcerns. The poet contradicts the Biblical view of human genesis that God created man in His image and proceeds to declare: "Humans were carved / in the image of flowers" (34). Gill indicates here that the theory of human genesis from God's own image is anthropomorphic, while his hindsight of human beings originating from nature (flowers) emphasises his belief that human beings are part of the ecocycle. However, the technological progress made by human beings is symbolically represented when the poet says, "Humans made wings / to sail above the rainbow clouds" and "created / their own plastic roses and jasmines / without roots" (34). The superficiality of their designs is coupled with zestless mechanisation by use of the figure of "robots." Notwithstanding these vacuous expansions, the poet foresees salvation for humanity only in its willing surrender to nature. He affirms:

> No matter
> what they do
> and what they think of themselves,
> humans still need
> the caring arms of the earth
> because they are
> flowers. (35)

In "Garden of Eden", Gill sees the protective power of "mother earth" as more powerful than the divine law. Because it sympathises with the exiled human beings and gives them refuge: "When Adam and Eve broke the sceptre of the divine law, / they were chased out from there; / only mother earth gave them refuge" (36). But Gill underscores the fact that Earth is the only planet that can seclude human beings and by spoiling it they will have nowhere else to go. As he points out:

> The blood of Cain
> still runs
> in the streams of the tree.
> It has poisoned
> the arteries of mother.
> Her fall
> would be the demise of an age.
> Her children
> will be soon exiled to another planet
> as their ancestors were.
> Where will they go from here
> is a question now. (37)

In "The Flower of the Universe", Gill communicates his ecoconcern in a figurative sense. He pictures a persona who, overpowered by possessiveness, crushes "the flower". However, appalled by a bleak vision of "a chaotic human crowd / under the darkening dust / of war, hatred and illusion," inside the stem, the persona attempts to reshape the flower with the realisation that the flower needs "the soft nurse of nature / and a mysterious rain" (38-39). In this way, the poet bespeaks of the redemptive power of nature and entails why it is all the more important to care for it.

"War Fever" is another poem that shows how "the demons of pollution" (47) cause ecological imbalance. In Gill's words: "War fever / poisons the air of surroundings / disturbs the calm of sea / crumbles human relations" (49). In "Year After Year", he sarcastically admonishes the incorrigible human tendency to selfishly consume natural resources for the present and leave its protection shamelessly to future generation. He remarks: "Abuse of the earth / ecosystem / legacy of garbage piles / we leave for posterity" (89). Similarly, "engulfed by the devils of technology," the persona of "Twentieth Century Says", evinces intense attentiveness to the depletion of the ozone layer owing to the capitalistic machinations. He notices: "the hands of commerce / frustrate their attempts / by polluting surroundings / with the acid rains" (96-97). Despite this thankless, self-centred, self-gratifying humankind, the poet is grateful to nature for it indiscriminately continues to shower human beings with its blessings. This is touchingly brought out in the poem, "Congratulations". The poet declares:

> I congratulate
> the freshness of the dawn
> for cheering cheerless hearts.
> I also congratulate
> the rain drops
> for effacing
> the futility of dryness
> from the womb of the earth;
> and the young branches
> for changing the mantle
> of the barren trees;
> and also the fire
> for strengthening the cowards;
> and above all
> the forge of friendship
> for producing meaning in life. (140)

Stephen Gill continues to express his ecoconcerns even in the recently published *Flashes* (2007). Although they are written in the Japanese condensed Haikuan spirit, they are pithy and even more effective. Especially, the poems written under "Social Concerns" carry forward the earlier ecomotifs. The following poem, for instance, juxtaposes the freshness of nature with the decomposed culture:

Morning mist
above the city graveyard
noises grow. (37)

But, soon the poet appears to be a bit pessimistic when he mourns because mankind that should serve and safeguard nature has gone against it and contributes to its annihilation. The anguish is felt when he speculates:

Gardeners trample flowers
who will feed birds
future ravaged. (37)

Ironically, the gardeners who are supposed to look after flowers endanger them. This is a clear warning of ecological disorder, as birds could not be fed by nature, which would subsequently devastate future livelihood.

Gill also laments for the world lost in commodified images that are enhanced by media and influenced by capitalist maneuvers. He bemoans: "Wasteland / charm / tv shows" (37). On the one hand, people are not interested in deriving pleasure out of watching greenery. On the other hand, they have already lost their abilities to derive pleasure by experiencing nature directly and their senses are so numbed that even televised pictures of wasteland charm them. Nevertheless, when the poet has lost hope of redeeming mankind, he trusts that nature will resort to its own methods of survival. In this respect, he is inclined to believe that the plants and other objects of ecosphere have a unified breathing consciousness, which to a large extent subscribes to Gaia hypothesis. As augmented by James Lovelock, Gaia hypothesis entails that "the entire range of living matter on Earth, from whales to viruses, and from oaks to algae, could be regarded as constituting a single living entity, capable of manipulating the Earth's atmosphere to suit its overall needs and endowed with faculties and powers far beyond of those of its constituent parts" (9). Thus, the following lines from *Flashes* are to be understood purely from the perspective of Gaia:

A tree in blossom
says something
breathes.

Only then, the green dove would soar towards eternity! And as Gill fittingly points out in "My Dove", "The leaf that she carries / is from the evergreen tree / of never ending hope" (*Shrine* 160).

Works Cited

Barry, Peter. *Beginning Theory: An Introduction to Literary and Cultural Theory.* Manchester University Press, 2002.

Gill, Stephen. *Flashes: Trilliums in Haiku Spirit.* New Delhi: Imprint, 2007.

________________. *Glimpses: A Selection of Published Articles About Stephen Gill and His Works.* Ontario: Vesta Publications Ltd., 2005.

________________. *Shrine: Poems of Social Concerns.* Arizona: World University Press, 1999.

________________. *Songs Before Shrine.* New Delhi: Authorspress, 2007.

Lovelock, James. *Gaia: A New Look at Life on Earth.* New York: Oxford University Press, 1987.

4

Sociation and Reghu Nath in Gill's *Immigrant*: A Study

—*G. Dominic Savio* and *S.J. Kala*

World into which one is born is wholly new at the time of birth. It is only through senses that one has the first experience of the world. These sensations facilitate building a view of the world. Communication takes place between the individual and others in society. The individual's action causes others to act forcing interaction to creep in.

Interaction, the core of social behaviour determines, human behaviour which can be well comprehended if one realises

> ... that the social actions of individuals are always oriented toward other human beings and that it is the interplay between the action of Self (Ego) and the expected or actual reaction of one or many others (Alters) which occupies the centre of the human stage. (Coser 65)

Interaction, therefore, involves norms, status positions and reciprocal obligations.

Despite the complex network that underlies various human behaviour in reality, many literary works deal with them. It never escapes the keen observation of creative writers who evince interest in delineating characters and their involvement in the phenomenon of interaction in the world created by them. Stephen Gill, an Indo-Canadian, a multi-faceted writer with deep insights and perception is no exception to it. Global peace and social concerns, his areas of interest, are conspicuous in his poems, novels, critical essays and children's stories. Upholding his belief that authors are obliged to improve the world, Gill's oeuvre is focused on contributing something to the society. His works are a sounding board for his social views.

> As a social researcher he applies his creative intuition to the condition of man to discover, what Niels Bohr calls, "the relations between the manifold aspects of our experience". (Singh 105)

With his first-hand experiences of an immigrant, he brilliantly records a new Canadian's plight in his second novel *Immigrant*, without missing out any detail of reality.

Brutal frankness in expression, various prejudices the Canadian society has in store for the new immigrants and a documentation of social value mark *Immigrant*. The novel effortlessly picturises the strife Reghu Nath, the persona, and his ilk face in the new country. Entrapped in a snare of racial discrimination, alienating culture, ethnic discrepancies, demanding professors, incomprehensible women and haunting memories of his motherland, Reghu Nath struggles desperately to interact with other human beings. The interplay between the action of Reghu Nath, the "Self" and the expected or the unexpected actions of many "Others" in Canada is the crux of *Immigrant*. This paper attempts at exploring the phenomenon of "Sociation" that Reghu Nath involves in, in a milieu full of contradictions, Canada.

"Sociation", the term is Kurt Wolff's rendering of Georg Simmel's German term, "Vergesellschaftung". As the literal translation of it, "Societalisation" sounds awkward and Albion Small's translation of the word as "Socialisation" has a specific meaning in sociology, sociologists most often use the word "sociation".

Georg Simmel, a philosopher, a sociologist and a co-founder of the sociological society is acclaimed as the founder of Formal Sociology. According to Simmel, an individual is a member of many specified groups of individuals and activities. A modern society, in his view, comprises of complex web of relations between individuals in constant interaction with one another, a thought that has introduced "Vergesellschaftung" or

"Sociation". Sociation is "the particular patterns and forms in which men associate and interact with one another" (Abraham 141).

The process of sociation that Reghu Nath, the protagonist of *Immigrant,* engages in as a grown-up man at an alien land is noteworthy. His relationship with other individuals, groups and masses is a painstaking effort towards sociation. His pattern of interaction is classified and analysed differentiating between "form" and "content" based on formal sociology. In the novel, "Form" – the basic structural configurations or that element in social life that is stable, is Reghu Nath's mode of interaction with other individuals. It refers to the "how" of social action in the novel. For Reghu Nath, Canada, the setting of the novel, is a land of greener pastures that he has sought after. Canadian nation with its multiplicity of cultures and its norms shape the behaviour of Reghu Nath. The metropolis of Ottawa and Montreal become the location for Reghu Nath's – the stranger (a social type) – interaction with others.

"Individual drives, purposes and other motive powers constitute the 'content'" (Abraham 142) of Reghu Nath's interaction. He, with the status of an immigrant, hunts for a job amid tight economic conditions. He chooses Canada as a home with aspirations for better opportunities and social well-being. Governed by loneliness, fear, apprehensions, nervousness, humiliation, antagonism and difficulty in adapting himself to a new life, he strives forward with the motive of gaining a dignified position in a hostile land.

Meanwhile, he shares his individual beliefs with those around him, who are part of the social world. Reghu Nath places himself in a social scale that depends on his frame of reference (North 51). His frame of reference is his *family* with mother, a brother and a sister. His *friends* and acquaintance circle comprises of Mary, Akram, Mrs. Patterson, Queen of Sheba, Mohan, Balwant, Sandy, Prabha, Mrs. Clifford, Dr. Hafeez, Mr. Aggarwal, Ron, a white friend, Mac and Grace. His *neighbourhood* encompasses Hollywood actress, Mrs. Wallace, Musician, Fatman and the Man in fifties. These people and those who work with him temporarily at schools, college, adfilms and the media introduce him to other groups of people. Reghu Nath's frame of reference can be diagrammatically represented as follows.

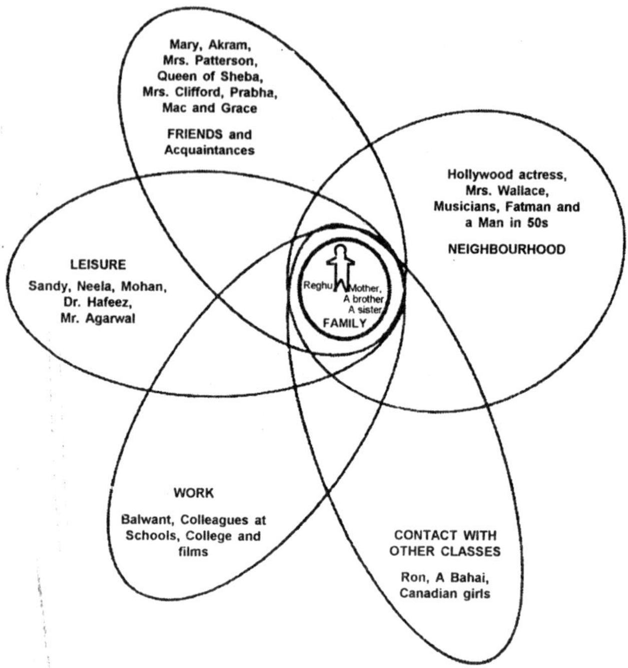

The frame of reference (North 52)

Reghu Nath's innumerable relationships with different types of people vary from a fleeting encounter with least significance to a relationship with an indelible impact on him. Out of the numerous forms of sociation classified by Simmel only three most important forms – Dyad, triad and superordination—subordination are used as guidelines to study the forms of sociation that Reghu Nath engages in.

Whenever, Reghu Nath interacts with another individual, Dyad, the simplest sociological formation operating between two elements is formed. The dyads in the novel can be analysed as those that are fleeting encounters, those that influence Reghu, those which allow him to express his individual beliefs and those that transform into a triad.

Most of the dyads formed are Reghu's fleeting encounters with other individuals. His encounters with the charming woman in VCIO flight to Montreal, receptionists in the overseas students' reception, officers at the International League Office, Canadian girls, the musician in his neighbourhood at Lorne Avenue, the Fatman and the Man in fifties who prod him to return to his country may be transitory but still they are sociation in themselves. They are prototypes of everyday experiences. Even these ephemeral engagements determine Reghu Nath's behaviour.

Besides these fleeting encounters there is yet another type of dyad in the novel that is quite far-reaching. Reghu's interaction with Akram, Mrs. Patterson, Queen of Sheba, Mrs. Wallace, girls of Indian origin, Dr. Hafeez and Aggarwal, fall under this category. Reghu meets Akram at the University library where both are employed on a part-time basis. It is Akram who exposes Reghu to the various nuances of a students' life in Canada.

> Akram's friendship proved to be useful to Reghu. He explained to Reghu about the health insurance plan of Ontario, the social security number, the credit system at the university, the methods of the university examinations, the purpose for term papers, and other things of which a newcomer from the sub continent of India is not aware. (17)

However, Reghu finds it hard to cope with the totally new situation.

In yet another dyad formed by Reghu Nath's interaction with a compatriot whom he meets within a few days of his arrival in Canada, he learns that clasping hands and walking hand in hand is a detestable behaviour in the West. "His newfound friend, already tuned into North American mores rejects Nath's gesture with a stern, 'This is not India'" (Westcott 104). After this incident, Reghu observes others and learns a lesson never to forget in his life. It even affects his own frequent habit of shaking hands warmly.

With new experiences Reghu moves further with the hope of establishing himself, when he meets Maple, a divorcee in her thirties, at the International League. She, an administrative secretary at a local college, waxes eloquence on her favourite topics – women, marriage and friendship. Her views on these controversial issues have a compelling impact on Reghu. Sporting jeans and craving for smoking and drinking, she presents herself as a by-product of modern civilisation that has robbed her of her emotions and natural impulses.

> Maple, on the other hand, considered sexual acquiescences obliging and felt the man should be grateful to her. (26)

Maple's behaviour and her controversial views do not appeal to Reghu Nath and so he severs his relationship with her. His secession destroys the dyad and a new one is formed in its stead with Mrs. Patterson, a 55-year-old divorcee from England coming closer to him.

Divorced twice, Mrs. Patterson feels very lonely and afraid of death but loves to hear eulogies of her physical and intellectual accomplishments. Having studied her well, Reghu never ceases to praise her. During the course of interaction with her, he discovers a friend, a mother, an aunt, and then a friend in her. By lending money and being helpful she exerts both positive and negative influences on him.

> He owed her his knowledge of Canada and its people, its politics, North American expressions, and his improved pronunciation. He was grateful to her for the confidence she built up in him. (27)

But, Mrs. Patterson's possessive and demanding nature has a negative impact on him, affecting his studies. The more Reghu tries to break away from her the more he feels very weak to ward off her influence.

The encompassing knowledge of Canada gained from Mrs. Patterson seems to be wanting when he meets Queen of Sheba. The formation of this new dyad helps him to trace the plight of the immigrants. She unlocks many truths about Canada that Reghu has never heard of.

> "Canadians will not give me the type of job for which I am qualified".
>
> "Why?'
>
> "Because they are prejudiced and suffer from the worst kind of inferiority complex. Believe me, Canadians will never give responsible positions to blacks easily" (44).

The interaction proves quite useful in throwing light on the darker side of Canada that is unknown to him.

His inquisitiveness to meet and interact with Mrs. Wallace, a freelance writer at the age of sixty, leads Reghu into a dyad. Undeterred by the fact that sex interests her more than money, his fascination for writers drives him into a relationship with her. His queries to her on the literary scene in Canada, particularly Montreal, and the status of successful writers there, expose him to the possibility of making a living by writing. Besides that he is jolted when she divulges a hard truth that Canada, a democratic nation, is in fact a Police state. By laying bare the details of how criminals escape and innocent citizens are always caught, Mrs. Wallace exposes him to hard realities. Knowledge of crime, Police, status of writers and a tip about the possibility of working in TV commercials is the highlight of this dyad.

Dyads of different natures are formed when Reghu interacts with Balwant, Neela and Prabha, all of Indian origin, and with Sandy, a Kenyan girl of Indian descent. Reghu meets Balwant, a tall, slim beautiful Hindu girl from Punjab at Royal Park during the shooting of a TV commercial. "Reghu was certain he would have a good time with Balwant to help him overcome the sharp pangs of life" (69). But, he gets disappointed when she turns out to be one who does not want to prolong friendship; she is rather interested in finding a suitable Indian boy who will marry her. Frustrated with this relationship he hunts for a friend who will not be obsessed with marriage and that is when he meets Sandy at a party.

Knowing well that Reghu is an Indian, she tries to demonstrate her identity by speaking in an Indian tongue. To his dismay, within two or three days, she too insists on getting married, forcing Reghu to evade her. Moving away from her he meets Neela, a nurse from India, at a party again, who is in no way different from Balwant and Sandy. She too nags him to get married. Escaping from all these quags he becomes cognizant of the intentions of the Indian girls in Canada whose prime desire is to get married and be settled in life.

Least interested in entangling himself in a lasting relationship, he bumps into Prabha, a cataloguer at the University Library. Unlike other Indian girls, she is not after marriage. "Reghu and Prabha met occasionally around the University, always talking about the indifference of Ottawans and antagonistic attitudes of some professors" (100). During their interaction with each other, Prabha discloses the discriminatory policy of the staff at the library. The dyad that emerges out of their friendship diminishes into nothing with the mysterious death of Prabha. The death, and the unbelievable account of it in the newspaper, confounds Reghu, traumatising him tremendously. "Reghu could not sleep the night he heard of Prabha's death. He felt lonely, a foreigner in a foreign land. The walls of his room closed on him" (105).

Despair constrains him to observe the same embitterment in Dr. Hafeez, a scientist from Bangladesh, whom he often meets on the streets of Ottawa. The pitiable and mysterious appearance of Dr. Hafeez lures Reghu into a conversation with him, ultimately a dyad evolves. Reghu gradually ascertains that Dr. Hafeez, a combustion engineer from British University, a professor, manages to find himself a position, with the department of chemical engineering at Canada. But, his brother's death in a car accident in Bangladesh forges Dr. Hafeez to give up his post. On his return to Canada, after six months, he does not get back the same position instead he has to live on unemployment benefit for eight months till he gets just a technical representative's position with an American lubricant company. Reghu is shaken up to know that even the present job of Dr. Hafeez necessitates "good public relations" (110),that he finds difficult in an unfavourable climate. The escalating dejection spurs Dr. Hafeez to return unwillingly to his native land, Bangladesh, though he hates her political climate. Reghu is altogether astounded, nevertheless, the dyad shapes his behaviour.

With the knowledge of Canada deduced from the dyads, Reghu finds an opportune moment to share his views of Canada with Mohan, an Indian, a newcomer to Canada. Reghu invites him for a drink and a chat, a fitting occasion for sociation. Reghu's open-minded and matured outlook of an immigrant surfaces out when he shares about Canada, its cultures and the girls. His tips on how to invite Canadian girls and a comparative study of them with their Indian counterparts exhibit his wide range of experiences.

> It is hard to bring them to your room and be intimate the first day. It is easier to lead an Indian girl into a compromising situation, though they take sex almost religiously...(65)

Reghu does not condemn Canadian culture. He tells Mohan that he sees no difference between men and women all over the world. Gill's concerns in universal brotherhood and World Federalism are manifested in this dyad.

Reghu's sociation with Prabha provides him with a chance to share his views on discrimination of some professors and the standard of education in Canada. He also discusses with her the prevailing combat between the members of the primary group comprising of the natives and the members of the secondary group, who are the outsiders.

Reghu's relationship with Aggarwal, yet another dyad, becomes a platform for Reghu to be on par with the other, the experienced immigrant in expressing his views on Canada. Aggarwal's condemnation of Christianity, unemployment, racial prejudices, and the system of education in Canada does not alter Reghu's attitude about the nation. His crude statement that Canadians consider Indians barbarians and non-cultured does not provoke Reghu. He responds in a well-thought-out fashion:

> It is unfair to make such a sweeping statement. As far as Christianity is concerned, it preaches love and tolerance. Many people cannot grasp this main message of Christ. For them, pride in so-called nationalism is above everything. They go to Church as a routine. Such persons exist in every nation and religion. You cannot condemn a religion for these bigots. (131)

A very long discourse with Aggarwal on varied topics inclusive of the rootlessness of his son makes Reghu mull over the stifling existence of immigrants, and he affirms that hatred, jealousy and discrimination are the upshot of ignorance.

Reghu then seizes the opportunity to talk with Ron, a white Canadian friend about Canadian Government and its political ties with India. Ron, a Bahai who believes in One World and One Government, relates with Reghu, forming a dyad. The dyad paves way for Reghu to boldly give his opinions on the immature decisions taken by the Canadian leaders in terminating the contract with the Government of India in nuclear supplies. During his conversation with Ron, Reghu appears to be the ambassador of India and its nuclear policies. His struggle to paint a true picture of India before Ron showcases his undying spirit of nationalism.

Some dyads refrain from being what they are and get transformed into triads, when a new member is added bringing in a profound structural change. The Dyad of Reghu and Akram changes into a triad when Akram's children are introduced to and interact with Reghu. The day Mrs. Wallace introduces Reghu to a woman, it turns out to be a triad. Begun as a dyad, Reghu's interaction with Prabha also grows into a triad when she introduces him to Mrs. Clifford who further brings in Judy and Ken into the triad.

A third element is introduced into the dyad and a triad is formed. The potentiality to exist on its own independent of each of its members makes a triad different from a dyad. The third party can take three basic roles as "(1) non-partisan mediator who seeks to be objective and not favor either side but help them reconcile their differences; (2) 'tertius gaudens' or being the third party who actually enjoys the conflict of the other two parties and seeks to use it for his or her own advantage; (3) divide and rule type of role in which the third party deliberately instigates conflict between the other two parties in order to promote his or her advantage" (Abraham 145).

Reghu and his interaction with Mary, her brother Dick and their parents who see him off at London Airport is the first instance of a triad in the novel. Mary's brother Dick and his parents do not seem to be closely related with Reghu, still they form a momentary group. This triad is just a passing mention in the novel, still the farewell at the airport is suggestive of a bond that binds them into a triad. The roles of the "third elements" in this momentary group cannot easily be identified and so classified into the three basic roles of the third party mentioned. It is obvious that Reghu's separation from the members of the triad does not dissolve the group. It continues in its own way perhaps with newer members in it.

A further reading of the novel confronts the reader with another triad comprising of Reghu, his brother, sister and mother. This group is a permanent group. The sociological function of the third party is not clearly studied because of the lack of relevant details about them as in the previous triad.

Reghu and Akram's sociation is a shift from a dyad to a triad. The "third party" in this triad is Akram's three "pretty little daughters, who call him uncle" (16). However, Akram felt lonely and sympathized with his children who were used to such an isolated life. It is indeed interesting to note how a dyad gradually shapes into a triad. Besides this, Akram's continual reference to Dr. Mernard perchance warrants Reghu's high regard for the professor.

Reghu's association with Prabha leads to the formation of a significant triad in the novel, with the addition of Mrs. Clifford as the third element. This sociological structure helps Reghu know more about motherhood and an old mother's anxiety of being lonely and deserted. The outpours of Mrs. Clifford on modernisation and its deadly impact bring to the fore the truth that machines have robbed them off their peace of mind.

> We've lost out feelings and sentiments, and have become as cold as our snow. Socially, we're dead...we no longer have blood in our veins. (101)

Towards the end of the novel, Reghu's association with Mac a businessman from India, and his white girlfriend, Grace, evolves into a triad. Mac is introduced to Reghu by an Indian whose wife worked as a salesgirl with Mac's garment shop. Reghu is not comfortable with Mac. Mac's deceitful practices lead Sanjay, Grace, Vachan and Dev Singh into bankruptcy, repelling Reghu from him. Yet, Reghu is forced into a relationship with him in the already formed dyad between Mac and Grace. Reghu, the third element, enters functioning as a "non-partisan" in the triad. Mac and Grace, the conflicting parties, after accusing "one another of infidelity and stealing money", reconcile with each other. The dissent between them is quite transitory. The "non-partisan" Reghu does not favour either of them yet the conflict comes to an end.

"Superordination-Subordination", the third major form of sociation in other words Simmel's sociology of power, materialises whenever Reghu, the subordinate, associates with his superiors in the society created by Stephen Gill. The Welfare Councillor offers Reghu a clerk's position at an office. The superordinate, the boss, does not exercise absolute authority or dominate over Reghu nor does he expect implicit obedience from his subordinate. "Domination of some form is a logical and structural necessity...." (Abraham 145) but when that is not found in its due proportion, the subordinates tend to fool around, make fun of and dodge the work.

> Everyone was provided with pencil and papers, which they kept in readiness. Whenever the boss passed, they would scribble something on the paper. Reghu drew, or made circles, and doodled meaningless figures. The third week the employees were filled with doubts and suppositions. One said, "the boss has a lot of work for us, but he doesn't know how to begin it". (35)

The employees come together as a group and they entertain themselves through games and puzzles. A high range of sociation takes place.

An altogether different kind of superordination is evident in the principal of a school with whom Reghu associates. It is only after enquiries made at a board in Sherbrooke and two or three calls to the principal that he reaches the school at Richmond to discover that the principal looks for a teacher who can speak French. Frustrated Reghu tries hard to explain to him how unjust they are in dismissing him on grounds that he does not know French, eligibility not specified in the advertisement. Besides exhibiting authoritative behaviour, he also labels him with the deficit which the 'inside group' actually has.

Later, Reghu encounters yet another principal of a college who has a striking resemblance to the one he has already met. This principal hunts only for a Canadian teacher which he openly declares to Reghu on the third day of their meeting. After wasting three days Reghu, the stranger, understands his role and position in this new society.

Reghu can be befittingly identified as a stranger, a social type. A gallery of social types—"the stranger", "the mediator", "the poor", the "the adventurer", "the miser", "the man in the middle", "the modern cynic" and "the renegade" —complements Simmel's inventory of a social forms. "The social type is a conception abstracted from the structural components of a particular social relationship and involves the essential qualities of the person as well as the awareness and expectation of the status role involved" (Abraham 146).

Reghu, the stranger, is the one who comes today and stays tomorrow. He "wanders" from one place to another in search of a suitable job. He tries his skills as a clerk, a teacher and an actor. Towards the end of the novel when Mac offers the position of a Cinema Manager, the readers feel that he will accept it and therefore there are more chances of his continuing his stay in Canada.

Reghu is a stranger as the place of his origin is India, a land of close family ties different from that of his host society, Canada. Reghu strives hard to establish strong bonds of relationships here but all in vain. There is also a marked difference in his independence in moving, the way of behaviour and the individuals of the society that he has entered.

It is to be comprehended that Reghu's position in this group is determined from the fact that he has not belonged to it from the beginning. Reghu becomes an element of the host society while not being fully part of it. He is labelled as a member of the outside group.

Having studied intensely the dyadic and triadic forms of Reghu Nath's sociation, the effects of sheer numerical size on them also need to be attended to. Throughout the novel, Reghu relates with people either in dyad or a triad, mostly dyad. The relationships comprising of just two, three or a maximum of five members result in influencing each other. Being a small group, Reghu, gets a chance to interact directly with one another. Face-to-face interaction takes place in most of the relationships, except his few telephonic conversations with Mrs. Wallace, the principal, and the secretary of the college. Face-to-face interaction is replaced by formal arrangements in a school/college where Reghu teaches and an office where he works. Since Reghu's sociation takes place in smaller groups, it is quite effective and influential.

Simmel's study of interaction specifically sociation has thus been helpful in analysing the phenomenon of sociation in Reghu Nath. The association of Reghu, "the stranger", through dyads, triads, superordination-subordination and the effect of the numerical size on the forms of sociation is worth a study as they "result in emergent social phenomena" (Turner 321). The study unearths the fact that sociation occurs not only in the lives of the members of the tangible society but also in lives of those like Reghu from the intangible society created by the novelist, that holds "the mirror up to nature."

Works Cited

Abraham, Francis and John Henry Morgan. *Sociological Thought from Comte to Sorokin*. Madras: Macmillan India.

Coser, Lewis A. and Bernard Rosenberg. *Sociological Theory: A Book of Readings*. New York: The Macmillan Company, 1959.

Gill, Stephen. *Immigrant*. Ontario: Vesta Publications Ltd., 1989.

North, P.J. *People in Society*. Essex: Longman Group Ltd., 1985.

Singh, R.K. "Cross Cultural Communication". *Language Forum*. Vol. XXIV. No. 1-2, Jan.–Dec. 1998.

Turner, Jonathan. H. *The Structure of Sociological Theory*. Jaipur: Rawat Publications, 1987.

Westcott, W.F. "Immigrant". *Christian Monitor*, Nov. 2, 1980.

5
Stephen Gill's *Life's Vagaries*: A Critique

—Ashok Kumar and *Roopali*

Short story, as a relevant branch of fiction, came to be recognised only in the middle of the nineteenth century. Though it existed in different forms in the past, as an art form it is something not very old. "It may be argued that the forefathers of the short story however rude in some cases are myth, legend, parable, fairy story, fable anecdote, exemplum, essay, character study, Marchen – not to mention the lai and fabliau and even the ballad".[1] Chaucer's *Canterbury Tales* and Boccacio's *Decameron* may also claim to be included in this new art form called short story.

The definition of short story has always been very elusive to the contemporary critics. Edgar Allan Poe, while reviewing Hawthorn's *Twice Told Tales* gave some general "serviceable precepts on the short story by which he meant a prose narrative requiring anything from a half-hour to one or two hours in its perusal; a short story that concentrates on a unique or single effect and one in which the totality of effect is the main objective."[2] Poe's definition may not hold ground today but it certainly gives some basis for useful discussion. But here we are evaluating a debutant short story writer, hence we shall concentrate on the matter and the narrative style of Stephen Gill.

Stephen Gill, who is of Indian origin and presently lives in Canada, has to his credit a collection of 14 short stories entitled *Life's Vagaries*. He has worked on W.B. Yeats' six plays and also composed poems of significant worth. But in the present critical analysis we shall be examining his collection of short stories. In general, when we take up any short story writer we start comparing him with Chekhov, Tolstoy and Maupassant which is not proper. In the present case we are not comparing Stephen Gill with the above-mentioned masters of the art of storytelling.

A short story deals with situations and concentrates on a single effect. In Mr. Stephen Gill's stories, men have been presented in different situations, and they behave as a man of this world. They are not the ideal figures. They are the real men of flesh and blood. They have in them the virtues and shortcomings of a common man. Mr. Dewar in the Preface of the book also confirms the above contentions:

> There are no traditional heroes or villains in his short stories; only real people reacting to the basic situations which are to be found in all corners of this global village.[3]

Daud Khan in "Pathan Soldier", Sita in "What a Mistake", Miss Lete the Eritrean girl in "The Younger Brother", Rejean the artist in "Determination" and Tom Murphy in "Contemporary Poet" are such protagonists who appear to be the inhabitants of the world in which we live. His protagonists are not like the ideal heroes of *Ramayana* or *Mahabharata*, they are the men and women of flesh and blood having human virtues and infirmities together.

In most of his stories the protagonist is placed in a difficult situation and he has to behave according to his social class. His stories may be placed in to two categories – (1) Stories of situation, (2) Stories of character. As the two categories denote, some stories hinge on situations and some on characters for the desired effect. To be brief, some stories are dramatic and some are character-centric. In some we find some suspense and we observe that the narrator withholds some fact or information to be revealed at the end. Some stories end with a surprising end. As we have mentioned earlier, we do not intend to compare Stephen Gill with the masters of the craft. But to determine his place, we may put him near Manohar Malgaonkar or Khushwant Singh. But the later mentioned Indian English writers are certainly better than Mr. Gill. However, Gill resembles them in skill to some extent.

The stories "Enigma", "Another Trap", "Two Votaries", "Aunt Disappears" and "Toys" are the stories which are very dramatic in nature, while "Death of a Dream", "Determination", "Pathan Soldier", "What a Mistake!" and "A Contemporary Poet" are character-centric stories. Some of the stories are neither situation-based nor character-based. These stories, founded on fine human emotions, touch the delicate chord of human sensibility. "London to Ottawa" and "Death of a Dream" are such stories.

Some of the character sketches carved by Gill are worth remembering, such as Daud Khan, Rajean, Miss Lete and Mrs. Rock. Some are odd and complex characters, such as Jack Kenneth, husband of Sita and Antonio. Though Gill's characters are not indepth studies, they appear real and convincing. Gill has succeeded in creating verisimilitude in his creations.

As discussed above, Gill has a knack for surprising his readers. This he has tried to accomplish through the technique of reversal. Aristotle calls it *peripeteia*. Robert L. Caserio, in his work *Plot, Story and the Novel* discusses it in relation to Charles Dickens and Sir Walter Scott:

> My answer is that at least as Dickens and his great predecessors Scott use reversal, peripety's representation of the instability of life incites the clearest and most persuasive reasoning and moralising of experience.[4]

Caserio also speaks of the significance of reversal for Aristotle:

> When Aristotle speaks of reversal and recognition as the soul of the plot and as the mark of the superior dramatist, he is favouring the power of turning point to engage the audience.[5]

Stephen Gill has also used reversal as a literary tool and has used it at the turning point to engage the readers. This technique is visible in "Aunt Disappears", "Enigma", "Two Votaries" and "A Pathan Soldier". The presence of disappeared aunt at the house of an ex-convict Ted, telling of Mrs. Rock to Antonio in "Enigma" ("I forgot to tell you that I am divorced") and the arrival of Lily in "Another Trap" are such master strokes which are the result of this technique.

As far as the contents of Gill's stories are concerned they come from the ordinary events of everyday life. The life which he observed at India, Ethiopia, Canada and Bangladesh provide a backdrop to his short stories. Down-to-earth realism can be observed by the readers in Gill's *Life's Vagaries*. The language which he employs is simple and has a natural ease which goes straight to the mind and heart of the reader. As a short story writer Stephen Gill shows a promising talent but many more miles he will have to tread before becoming a master craftsman.

References

1. J.A. Cuddon, *A Dictionary of Literary Terms*, Penguin Books, New York, USA, Reprint 1984, p.623.
2. Ibid., p.623.
3. Stephen Gill, *Life's Vagaries*, Vesta, Canada, 1974, p.11.
4. Robert L. Caserio, *Plot, Story and the Novel*, Princeton University Press, 1979, p.57.
5. Ibid., p.67.

6

Seeking the Dove of Peace: The Poetry of Stephen Gill

—Sailendra Narayan Tripathy

A homeless beggar
I wander
to catch a glimpse of reality
from different angles
on the pieces of glass. ("Self", *Shrine*)

I am no admirer of political or realistic poetry. I was somewhat sceptical, when I started reading the verse of Stephen Gill—the Sialkot-born poet, who grew up in India, saw the horrendous bloodshed of partition and carried the scars to Ethiopia, Britain and Canada, where he is much-adored and settled.

Gill is ageless. So is his poetry. I read his poems mostly in the verdant glory of my village, with the aroma of mango blossoms seducing me deeper into the world of Gill.

I must confess *Shrine*, his collection, gripped me like an Octopus. He has a long introduction which he could have done without. But the biographical details help us to understand more of his poetry and of course his vision.

Wasn't Yeats a political poet? What about the plays of Arnold Wesker? What about Osborne's *Look Back In Anger*? Or the poems of Sengher or Nobel Prize winner Zymberska?

A poet is born and bred in society. He is deeply influenced by the flotsam and jetsam of history. T.S. Eliot's epoch-making essay "Tradition and Individual Talent" so eloquently talks about the writer's debt to history. Even Gill says, "A person is largely the product of the environment."

Shrine is the poet's reaction to the tumultuous events of history; all that overtook him and a trail of scars left on the good earth.

> It
> brings darkness to the mind
> spoils the taste of happiness
> mutilates the body of humanity,
> compelling
> the worship of violence
> seizure of sons from mothers
> and
> the cultivation of thorns. ("War Fever")

There are veiled hints and suggestions to the bloodbath, history witnessed during the partition years of India-Pakistan.

Like the swan in Yeats poetry, Gill's dominant image is that of dove, which stands for world peace. But the dove is under threat:

> Sleeping in the web of greed
> arms traders forget the dove
> hidden in caves of blood. ("Arms Traders")

The dove of peace lies in tatters. The dove is intimidated by the "hounds of war" and is smeared in blood.

> The dove pleads
> that the dance of the hounds
> be stopped
> to let her pacifying carol
> fortify human muscles
> to build more Taj Mahals
> and pyramids of justice. ("Hounds Of War")

Bloodshed, violence, the bleeding dove, the arms traders, the hounds of war are not the only problems gripping Gill. His poetry unravels the democratic vistas. He dreams of flowers of democracy blooming everywhere in the world. There is no gainsaying the fact that Gill at heart is a humanist, and he wants happiness and peace of mankind. In the poem "My Beliefs", he makes it clear what would be his vision and peace is the ultimate goal of life. To reach that goal, mankind needs a democratic vision:

> I rather believe
> famine is man-made
> and sunshine a child of peace. ("My Beliefs")

He is totally against the sword, the bullet or the bomb. He had a surfeit of it in his childhood, which is soaked in blood.

> Those who kiss
> the lips of the sword
> fall victims to its fury. ("Convictions")

The rise of fundamentalism and the despotic rules and the walls of mistrust fill him with anguish:

> I am a human
> I love human kind.
> Smile, my friend
> because
> we are all one. ("I Am Still A Man")

There are existential anxieties and angst of a nuclear holocaust of a third world war:

> If the nuclear bombs drop
> Will the buds bloom again?
> Will the birds chirp again?
> Will the spring return again? ("A Question")

But what left me haunted is a poem addressed to his mother, whom he left in the prime of his youth, never to see her again:

> Years have gone by still
> I see your tearful eyes
> and catch the choking moans
> coming from the crumbling pyramid
> of pains. ("To Mother")

That is vintage Gill; the magical mixture of moods, music, and memories. Didn't P.B.Shelley say, "A poet is an uncrowned legislator of mankind"? Gill belongs to that bardic race. Like Whitman he sings of man. That is the oldest song of the world.

Books Cited

Gill, Stephen. *Shrine*. Arizona: World Universities Press, 1999.

________________. *Songs Before Shrine*. New Delhi: Authorspress, 2007.

7

"In the Fire of Self": A Critique of Stephen Gill's *Shrine*

—Kanwar Dinesh Singh

On the passage to realisation and recognition of his true "self", Stephen Gill seeks some sort of withdrawal from the outer distorted and disconcerting realities to his inner world, which is the world of his conscience, his scruple, his imagination, his contemplation, his real self that lies in the dark, yet unexplored. Now he feels the need to be with his own self, to peer into himself, to talk to himself, to listen to himself, to express himself and to radiate his own self. Nevertheless, this search for one's inner self is the dire need of the hour.

Every man needs to explore and actuate his/her real self. It is only with the actuation of one's rightful self that a healing change can be brought about in today's ailing humanity. "Self" is the building block of the world and so holds a place of great importance. Any kind of flaw in any one of the "selves" may distort the very edifice of the world. So, it is always imperative for every individual to keep an eye on one's "self" to maintain its due configurations and proportions. Such a task is being endeavoured by the conscientious poet in Gill, as pronounced in his poem "Me":

Today
I want to be me;
I wish to sing my own song . . .
In the fire of self
let me radiate . . .
I want to express my self . . . (30-31).

There is no egotism in the poet's words as such there is the very emotion for the essentiality and expressivity of the genuine self. The search for one's true self is, none the less, the beginning of finding eternity.

According to the poet, "self" is too brittle, wavering and prone to be astray in the fluid and unpredictable circumstances of today. The "self" needs to be checked, safeguarded, restrained and steadied. The poet tries constantly to ascertain the existence and endurance of his self *vis-à-vis* changing values in the changing world. In "Self", he reveals:

Every day
I check the mirror
to be sure
if the reflection is mine. (44).

Many a time, his conscience remains silent at the coarse circumstances and heartless stance of the modern man. In the poem entitled "Conversation", Gill asks his conscience "if it had perceived / in the eyes of humankind / the unshed tears / of hurt and humiliation", but he found that his conscience "dozed / like the indifferent gods / on high mountains", and soon he gets at its speechlessness: "Its trembling lips / were an ocean of truth / which revealed to me that / conscience is blessed / with everything, / except words" (40-41). Indeed, today's state of affairs is too appalling, atrocious and upsetting that one's conscience is silenced, almost anesthetised. In several poems of *Shrine*, Gill has movingly delineated the wretched and abject condition of the contemporary world, which has shocked and shaken his conscience.

At several places in *Shrine*, Gill has ridiculed the human deportment toward nature. He feels that human beings are foolish to divide, control and claim possessively the objects of nature, which have been provided to them by God to share in common. In the poem "Who Shall Buy?", Stephen Gill tries to establish that nature enjoys dignity and freedom in herself and this freedom can never and no how be bought or sold or usurped by anyone for the entire nature is the creation of the divine and not that of earthly beings, and thence cannot be enthralled by anyone belonging to this mortal world:

No one can buy
Nor sell . . .
the blessings of the skies,

the warmth of the valleys,
the freedom of the winds,
the grace of the lakes,
the dignity of the palm trees,
the mystery of the oceans,
the sobriety of the jungles,
. . . the songs of the seasons,
the fragrance of the flowers,
the interdependence
of all animals, nations and nature . . . (32-33)

Stephen Gill employs certain Biblical images accentuating the present day predicament of man in the poem "Garden of Eden". He believes that the cause of all human misery is man himself. It is all due to the wrongdoings of man that he suffers on earth. Ever since the felony of Adam and Eve, the blunders could not be rectified. Though Mother Earth provides the refuge:

When Adam and Eve
broke the sceptre of the divine law,
they were chased out from there;
only mother earth gave them refuge. (36)

In these lines, one can find a momentous blend of the Christian and the Hindu beliefs, one in the myth of Adam and Eve and the other in having the sense/spirit of gratitude towards Mother Earth respectively.

In several of his poems, Stephen Gill thematises human strife with nature. Man seems to be conceitedly contesting against nature, without realising that man is dependent on nature only for his sustenance. Gill's ecological vision depicts man as an offshoot of nature alone, which nourishes and nurses human being as mother, condoning the misdemeanours of her children. Human beings are always dependent on nature for her motherly care and concern: "No matter / what they do / and what they think of themselves, / humans still need / the caring arms of the earth . . ." (34). The poet thinks that human beings must correct their demeanour or they are doomed. Earth as mother has always been considerate and compassionate to man. Even when, for committing a sin, Adam and Eve were ousted from the Garden of Eden, "only mother earth gave them refuge" out of her benevolent nature.

The poet feels deeply concerned for the belligerence between one human being and another. According to Gill, the bounties of nature are equal for one and all, and since there is no discrimination in nature, why should it be in the human world. He holds that humans must realise, appreciate and acknowledge symbiotic interdependence between one human being and another as they "breathe / the same air / under the same canopy" (32), and thus they must adorn the human world with grace, dignity, sobriety, fragrance, freedom and amity. The reasons for which human beings fight against each other are too trivial, emerging out of self-conceit and narrow self-centred vision. In fact, all human knowledge is flawed, leading to false ego and rivalry: "they planted / the seed of the tree of knowledge" which has "yielded the fruit of / jealousy, superiority, murders, / rapes and exploitation" (36). The human beings have forgotten that they are all brethren as they are all offspring of the same mother Earth. The Cain struggle pains and troubles the mother: "It has poisoned / the arteries of mother." (37). The poet warns the self-seeking humans: Her fall / would be the demise of an age." (37).

The poet shows profound concern for peace which is constantly under threat from warfare. He calls the modern world a "civilization of thorns" (49). In fact, war "crumbles human relations" and obliterates humanity, love, innocence, happiness, truth, harmony, melody, comfort, peace, calm, truth, mind and soul. The poet is disturbed even by the thought of war, which takes him into a closet of dread and anxiety. The news of warfare and its aftermath shown on the television is nightmarish and horrendous: "Women crying / around debris, / men hurling abuses / children confused and despaired . . . ." (54). In empathy, the poet feels himself to be a hostage to the brutal, inhuman forces:

> Alert in the bunker of panic
> I lie a hostage
> to the ghastly Gulf War
> that raises
> the high walls of captivity
> to my freedom and peace
> in my own living room
> though I am thousands of miles
> afar. (53)

In "Talking of Peace", the poet asserts that peace cannot be achieved merely by talking of it; though every one wants, it, envisions it and craves it, but it shall remain a dream until all come forward against war, weaponry, terror, tension, crime and cruelty. The rulers, leaders, politicians, and citizens, all talk of peace, but it is futile as long as "nuclear-powered marines / sail over breasts of the oceans / missiles look down as hawks / and neutrons / make fun of every life . . . / . . . citizens are locked / in the prison of their fears . . . / . . . homes are destroyed / by tensions of human relations . . . / the crop of the arsenal is raised / and the demons of pollution / stand tormenting us. / . . . there is no accounting / of criminals; / and the subjects are dominated / by the cruelty of the autocrats" (46-48).

Akin to most of the expatriate poets, a feeling of nostalgia, insecurity and mal-adjustment in an exotic atmosphere strikes even Stephen Gill. In poems like "To Humanists", "Refugees", "An Immigrant Complains", "Go Back", etc., he explicates the predicament and paranoia of the expatriates. The conflict arises when the natives claim to be possessive about their motherland forgetting that the earth belongs equally to one and all. With a Biblical allusion he tells the native who asks him to go back to his own country:

> Do not tell me to anywhere,
> my friend.
> This is our land
> where our father lives.
> We are all in exile. (81)

What aches the poet is the splitting up of humanity by reason of egocentrism, ignorance, doubt, negation and lack of understanding. Humanity is endangered "beneath the filth / of racial theories / and / in the cracks of social ladders" (87). Violence, apartheid, racial discrimination, communalism, hooliganism, larceny, crime, scorn, spite and differences in the society of today deride humanity and its Creator. Stephen Gill writes: "Humanity is torn asunder. / It has carved / disorderly islands: / each an empty tomb of notions. / These / self-surrounding cells of egoism / display the nudity / of modern savagery" (83). Indeed, it is the bloated ego and self-interest only that is behind most of the ills of contemporary society.

Depicting the condition of the refugees in an alien country, Gill states: "I have gazed / into the graveyard of their eyes / . . . / Those guests of humanity / I see emerging / from one cave / to shelter in another / . . . / A smoke of uncertainty / surrounds them like fear / and the albatross of loneliness / sits upon them / like a paperweight" (76). The refugees being "guests of humanity" are given an inhuman treatment in the land where they seek shelter and love. They are bogged down by apathy, bigotry, loneliness, emptiness, discomfort, ache, misery and injustice. The condition of the refugees on a foreign land is really pathetic and deplorable: "In the furnace / of their helplessness / they burn themselves, / not knowing / it turns them into ashes / beneath the snow / of their hopeless surroundings" (77).

The present-day world, as depicted by Stephen Gill, is ridden by chaos, anarchy, violence, animosity, killings, pillage, fights, famine, starvation, want, poverty, malnutrition, disease / epidemic, medicine scarcity, untimely deaths, stress, exhaustion, refugee camps, differences, disharmony, ethnic feuds, lust, intolerance, bigotry, slight, injustice, ignorance, erroneous notions and assumptions, lack of sympathy and understanding, etc. The familiar sight of the world of today comprises "open mass graves", "grenades . . . thrown in places of worship", "religions . . . taken to the streets", "drops of blood", "cries of the wounded", "In half-shut eyes / their dreams are now stones", etc. And what is even more distressing is that "The earth / that drank their blood / is speechless . . . ." (68-71).

Even a number of religious faiths do not have any cure for the ailing humanity of today. Rather, these religions are dragging human beings poles apart. In fact, religious fanaticism is another curse for the humankind. It is merely due to petty selfish interests and ignorance that people are turning diametrically opposed in the name of religion. Gill calls fanaticism as "bearer of deformed urchins / in the ruins of assumptions" and spells out the reasons behind its growth:

> It grows
> on the Babel of confusion
> in the lap of
> the blinding dust of vanity
> by the arrogant prince of ignorance. (63)

Nevertheless, today's world is heading unto democracy, but the democratic values of freedom, equality, peace, harmony, understanding, social justice and self-governance are threatened by fascist and sadistic forces. But all dangers can be overcome by the "will of the masses", so hopes Gill. Democracy has the innate strength to prevail over all odds and evils, and it proclaims: "as a tower of trust I stand / in the vastness of fuming waves. / I am aware of the dangers . . . / I know I am surrounded / by the demons of insanity. / Still I fight alone / holding the shield of light . . . / With my own strength / and patience / I shall continue postponing / each Armageddon." (57-58)

It is, undoubtedly, high time to ponder over the future of humanity. The twentieth century has been "the father of conflicts / . . . pointless struggles . . . / Under the sky of the soulless glitter" (96), but it is time for everyone to find out some resolve for the ongoing crisis. In the poem "Legacy", the poet conveys how "Today" warns of the impending danger:

> I am Today;
> . . .
> I have planted in my yard
> the trees
> which give the fruits of pain,
> fear, loneliness
> and self-destruction. (92-93)

Shrine is the document carrying woes of the victims of life in the modern world. A desire for love, harmony and peace is the repeated end in this volume beside the motifs of alienation, loneliness, insecurity, fear, pain, suffering, disease, hunger, despair, anger, cruelty, discrimination, injustice, sex-abuse, terrorism, warfare and several other conflicts of the today's world. In "Will of the Masses", the poet pronounces hope that the common masses have the power to transform the circumstances provided they come together and assert their strong will. It was the "will of the masses" alone that had "emerged / in the Vietnam war; / brought down / the walls of Berlin; / crushed terror / in Romania overnight" (65). The will of the masses rambles "like the leaves of autumn", and simmers within like a "silent volcano", and when aroused it turns subversive and before its might "even the earth yields" (66). The poet has every hope that the will of the masses would certainly bring about a radical change in the circumstances from which the present humanity is suffering, for it proclaims: "Cruelty cannot kill me" (66). Though it is so unassuming and simple-hearted that it can be pleased and swayed by affability and humility:

> I am ice;
> anyone can look into me.
> Warmth melts me. (65)

In all, there prevails some sort of open-endedness in most of the poems in this collection. At places, the poet appears to be writing as a news-reporter in the field relating the events and incidents happening around while the public is looking on silently, helplessly and gapingly. In fact, these poems are rather question-tags put to readers expecting them to ponder over and find out the pertinent resolves for the ongoing crisis in the human world. Some of the remarkable features of these poems are: the verbal felicity and flow,narrative continuity, effortlessness in phraseology, genuineness of feeling, conviviality and lack of artifice.

Work Cited

Gill, Stephen. *Shrine*. Arizona: World University Press, 1999. All subsequent references to this work have been parenthetically incorporated within the text.

8

Stephen Gill's *Immigrant*: A Study in Diasporic Consciousness

—*Nilofar Akhtar*

The phenomena of diaspora and expatriation are by all means an old one. However, its impact in the present times is larger and deeper. It has become a contemporary social trait and also a literary genre. The growing incidence of the diaspora has given place to dislocation, disintegration, dispossession and disbelongingness. The experience of expatriation not only gradually disconnects the individual from his roots, simultaneously it polarises his existence, which straddles between nationality and exile.

Here, at the onset it will only be apt to bring into light the historical significance of the diaspora. All serious study of diaspora traces its history way back with ethnic Jewish model of diaspora. However, the term is widely used now for all the activities of expatriation, which lead to emotional and physical displacement. The modern Indian diaspora began in the later half of the nineteenth century and counts for the bigwigs like Salman Rushdie and V.S. Naipaul. Stephen Gill is an India-born Canadian writer who has successfully portrayed the diasporic consciousness of an immigrant who came to Canada in search for greener pastures and in the process physically and culturally alienates himself from his native place. His disillusionment is complete when he finds no takers of talent and qualifications. His cultural affinity with India makes him an alien in Canada where he makes repeated attempts to transmute and transform his identity.

Diaspora therefore is an emotional and psychological state of (a) strutting between two geographical and cultural states (b) struggling between regression and progression, dislocation and then, relocation. This continuum of perpetual shift between two states of dislocation and relocation makes one interrogate the sustainability of an individual in such a situation. Diaspora relates to history and culture and this experience of inhabiting two history specific and culture specific spaces yields to subtle tension of dislocation and alienation. The strategy that accounts for such cultural shock of a migrant as that he tries to construct multiple identity and develops a hybrid vision, which eventually becomes an ongoing process for adaptation.

In an essay published in the 80's, Salman Rushdie has brought out the agony and the ecstasy of being an expatriate:

> Exiles or immigrants or expatriates are haunted by some sense of loss, some urge to reclaim, to look back, even at the risk of being mutated into pillars of salt.[1]

He shares his own diasporic experience, thus:

> But if we do look back, we must also do so, in the profound knowledge — which gives rise to profound uncertainties — that our physical alienation from India almost inevitably means that we will not be capable of reclaiming precisely the thing that was lost; that we will, in short, create fictions not actual cities or villages, but invisible ones, imaginary homelands, India of the mind.[2]

Stephen Gill has depicted, in his novel, this hybridity of the 'immigrant' who is strutting across two spaces — geographical and cultural. He is looking forward towards the country of his settlement for acceptance and involvement and simultaneously, yearning for his 'imaginary homeland'. With a backward glance, he moves on. Reghu Nath, the immigrant lives in Canada out of an option but never rules out the prospects of return. He opts for a migrant status in Canada and chooses to be an immigrant. However he could not break away clean from his own culture and carries the 'cultural baggage' with him.

His past experience as an Indian and his present status as a Canadian bring him close to socioeconomic and political contradictions. He understands the strategy of cultural sharing *vis-a-vis* survival in a new environment. As a highly qualified Indian, he finds himself unable to get a good job in Canada and feeds on local welfare schemes.

> Reghu grew more and more restless and worried with the passage of time. The more he considered the future and his security, the more nervous he became. He hated the idea of being a parasite on society by living on welfare. The way it was

> handled was humiliating and disdainful. Even the man at the welfare office behaved as if he were doling out money to robbers under sheer compulsion. There seemed no mutual respect and understanding between the recipients and the office staff.[3]

Reghu Nath becomes a victim of such socioeconomic and political contradictions which give rise to (a) either marginalisation of cultures or, (b) cross cultural communication (which is a milder expression of submission). An immigrant is constantly in pulls and pressures and suffers a marginalised existence as he carries with himself, the 'cultural baggage' of his ' homeland', which exists only in the figment of his imagination.

What I am attempting to formulate in this essay are the diaspora sensibilities of an Indian student in Canada, where he tries to build strategies of cultural identification. Gill, like other writers of the diaspora, has narrated these experiences in a wide range of his literary narratives. It might be interesting to note that around thirty of notable writers of India are either settled in U.K., U.S.A., Canada and so on or keep shifting base between India and abroad. Stephen Gill reflects upon the issues of expatriation in a way which is different from other practioners of diasporic writings. In the case of Reghu Nath, who moves away from India to Canada, in the process accentuates both a sense of loss and cultural and geographical alienation. He tries to deracinate himself but fails. His appearance, language, accent, knowledge, every aspect of his personality betrays him in Canada.

> Reghu knew that he spoke English with an accent. Whenever he thought of it, he felt ashamed, considering the time he had spent on his studying in India to be partly wasted. His teachers all Indians, never bothered to correct his pronunciation. Perhaps they had the same problem.... His command of a wide vocabulary did not help him; on the contrary, it impeded his conversation as he paused to determine which word was the appropriate one to use.[4]

As an immigrant, Reghu is caught between identity crisis and cross-cultural communication and as a consequence develops a double vision, a hybrid glance to combat such a marginalised existence. Salman Rushdie, in his essay 'Imaginary Homelands' has reflected on this issue, thus:

> Our identity is at once plural and partial. Sometimes we feel we straddle two cultures; at other times, that we fall between two stools .... But however ambiguous and shifting this ground may

> be it is not an infertile territory for a writer to occupy. If literature is in part the business of finding new angles at which to enter reality, then once again our distance, our long geographical perspective, may provide us with such angles.[5]

Thus, an immigrant 'falls between two stools' and perceives actions, events and experience in a relative light. This openness of perception and double vision comes as a by-product of diaspora and helps an expatriate to make the recognition that the world is an open platform where different interpretation of one action / event / experience may be possible. Gill sees the predicament of Reghu from political angle, too and apprehends Canadians' policy of exclusion as a desperate bid to tarnish the image of Canada. At the other end, Gill also makes Reghu see all the discrepancies which are prevalent in his own country hampering its progress, thereby. His long sojourn away from home brings into him a perpetual physical and emotional dislocation, which signifies his diasporic consciousness. His long physical absence from India makes him see through things. He understands that there are advantages of being positioned at a distance from ones own country. For one, he could now see that reality is a relative term and it is coloured by our personal likings and aversions.

> Reghu was driven to thinking about his own country, where he had held a good position before coming to Canada. It would be hard to return to find another job in his country, which was beset with problems of its own.[6]

An immigrant draws on two distinct cultural modes and is caught between two sets of ideologies — walking across two terrains, dwelling much on either side and in the attempt disrupting long established epistemological notions. Thus, Reghu Nath ruminates over socio-political issues of India and Canada.

> The thing about India that pained him most was the mockery of democracy. But then this mockery existed in one form or another, in all countries. Reghu scrutinised different corners of the globe to find one spot where the ugly head of mockery had not risen. Soon he realised that every region and nation has been plagued by its people's narrow mindedness and prejudices, the difference only in degree and kind. With that Reghu's eyes grew heavy. He fell asleep, his thoughts settling on the determination to stay in Canada, the land he would adopt and love by choice, not by accident.[7]

Reghu's opting for Canada over India is a tell tale sign of diasporic consciousness which is increasing fast, today. Post-independence, there has been a rampant growth in the rate of immigration in tandem with growing rate of foreign investment and advancement of information technology yielding much to the new concept of 'global trotting'.

A diasporic writer as the global trotter operates from out side India giving authentic literary representations of their diasporic consciousness. An Indian national emigrates in order to have better job prospects and excellent quality of life. For this purpose, he foregoes his home, society and nationality. He finds lacunas in the so-called legal, social, economic and political set ups of his country with a dire urge to succeed and obtain the much coveted NRI status, he leaves behind his home and chooses exile. The act of immigration has socio political implications as well. Some find Indian tradition and culture suffocating and look forward to a more liberal society where there are less or absolutely no social / sexual mores. But, this new environment also brings them the cultural shock and they are left bewildered and uprooted at the indenture of their new abode. However, very few return to India even after their disenchantment is complete. Thus, the concept of 'home' becomes a nostalgia, a pleasant reminiscence of the past which is ideal but never real. There are still some who retain their native connection and live in the country of their choice without loosing touch with their own culture. Reghu, as an expatriate decides to stay back (like his author who has narrated such diasporic experiences through his writings — poems, travelogue and fiction).

Reghu is conscious of his diasporic existence which means that he suffers from dislocation, dispossession, alienation, hybridity and above all dissatisfaction on 'not belonging to' the new country. 'Unbelongingness' is made a virtue, a celebration of his diasporic existence and he accepts it in order to survive in the centre margin construct which is constituted on the binary notions of master / slave, imperial / colonial, coloured / white, we / the other.

Then, the issue of identity forms the core of the diasporic consciousness of Reghu. He meets ill treatment and racial slurs at the hands of the Canadians. The moment one becomes an expatriate, he needs to define himself as the new environment compels him to do so. In this attempt of self definition one may either assimilate his identity with his host country thereby severing all ties with his native country, or he may resume his Indianness and see the people around as 'the other'. Cultural assimilation and cultural alienation are the two extremes within which an expatriate tries to adjust himself. Reghu too experiences this confusion of contrasting values and submits to his new environment by adopting the strategy of "excessive belonging". He concludes that human beings were basically alike everywhere.

> Men and women all over the world are the same basically. These so called cultures are man made and cause confusion and anarchy. A university bred girl from India can be a worse wife than a Canadian educated girl.[8]

He uses this strategy of excessive belonging in order to gain ground in a new milieu and interrogates the concept of nation and nationality.

For an expatriate, 'home' is a recurrent theme as Indians are more attached to its concept. In Reghu's case, living abroad for long, he suffers a break up with family and loses a sense of protection which it provides. Neither can he go back for he is short of money. Between home and exile, there is a tight rope walking for him which makes him revert to the strategy of 'excessive belongingness'. With globalisation, more and more people are moving from one part of the world to another. They now prefer 'to gravel' than to 'be home'. Like Reghu, people are leaving their secured home for 'the journey outward'. Disillusioned, they might be but are least willing to go back. Reghu understands such contemporary cosmopolitan trend of dislocation where 'centrality' and 'marginality' have blurred and overlapped each other. He is against any kind of centre be it colonial or national and favours 'decentring' much like his narrator. Dismissive towards the concept of culture, nation and nationality, 'the immigrant' advocates the formation of new cultural configurations, which may help in the assimilation, and understanding of divergent groups and societies.

References

1. Salman Rushdie, "The Indian Writer in England", *The Eye of the Beholder. Indian writing in English*, ed. M. Butcher (London: Common Wealth Institute, 1983), p. 83.
2. Ibid., 83.
3. Stephen Gill, *Immigrant* (Ontario: Vesta, 1982), p 79.
4. Ibid., p.19.
5. Salman Rushdie, "Imaginary Homelands", *London Review of Books*, 7-20, October, 1982, p.18.
6. Stephen Gill, *Immigrant*, p.33.
7. Ibid., p.34.
8. Ibid., p.66.

9

Paradoxes in the Works of Stephen Gill

—Nikola Dimitrov

Immigrant, a novel by Stephen Gill, is about peace, equality, human rights, freedoms, and about the quest for relationship, intimacy, as well as about the craftiness of the world's systems, the mundane life, and about the plague of ignorance. The novel is also about discrimination.

People are discriminated against everywhere and about anything with only slight variances. Anyone who is a little different to the existing identity may become an object of discrimination. Stephen Gill gives an example in the Preface to his collection of poems *Shrine*:

> In 1947, shortly before and after the partition of India, the Hindus, Muslims and Sikhs got involved with killing each other. The Hindus and Sikhs were on one side and Muslims on the other. Humans were killed in the midst of a crowd because they happened to look different because of their dress or shaving pattern.[1]

Billions of people in the world are discriminated against in various forms, including physical, verbal and mental abuse and even death. This is one of the most stupid paradoxes, because the Creator has made every being in His own image and likeness. Who authorises some humans to consider themselves superior to others on the basis of colour, intellect, place of birth, social, political and financial status? Life has become miserable because humans attempt to be equal to God.

War is also the outcome of discrimination and prejudice. Since the time of the creation of the world, there have been wars between brothers, families, cultures, ethnic groups and nations. Scholars can give several explanations and reasons for wars, but to look at from a pure humanistic point, war is a paradox that is born because of the pride and lust for money and power and also because of ignorance. Wars are fought even to obtain peace, independence, democracy and security. But wars have brought nothing, except destruction. Wars have been crippling people, affecting the spirit, soul, emotions, and educational, political and economic systems of every nation. Their effects continue for generations. This is what Stephen Gill tries to point out, particularly in his poem "About War": "war/ sheer fraud/ war chokes the joy of life/ victor and loser suffer / it kills man's hopes/ bringing destruction to all."[2] In another poem "War Fever", he says:

> War fever
> poisons the air of surroundings
> disturbs the calm of the sea
> crumbles human relations
> kills the appetite of the soul
> weakens the lover of love,
> turning everything upside down.[3]

My own nation – Bulgaria— has been in wars and bondages ever since its foundation. Bulgarians have come from the famous Kazaks in distant Asia, mixed with different tribes in Europe and produced mighty warriors of their time. Within its existence of 1326 years as a nation (681 – 2007), Bulgaria has been free for less than 200 years. When the final bondage of Communism fell in 1989, the country became so much devastated that it would take now generations to recuperate. Most people have no idea about a computer, internet, to say the least about business opportunities, creative thinking, higher education, science, technology, health care, and so on. The whole generation that Moses led through the wilderness, had to die, because of their mentality. They could not reach the promised land. Wars bring bondages and slavish thinking — serious obstacles on the path to enter the promised land of prosperity, joy and peace.

Bulgaria entered the European Union at the beginning of 2007. Now Bulgaria has a tremendous opportunity to be a great nation. However, there is not much progress in this direction. The difference between eastern and western Europe is vast, because of the mentality. It is almost impossible to keep the young people in within Bulgaria, because, to realise their potential, they want to go abroad and study and work in a more developed nation. This robs Bulgaria of the most valuable resource. There is absolutely nothing good in it and still people wage wars, forgetting peace that brings prosperity. War is definitely a paradox.

The Bible defines the Lord as the God of Peace in the book of Judges 6:24.[4] This is the kind of peace that results from being a whole person in the right relationship with God and to one's fellow beings. In the *New Testament*, apostle Paul calls the Lord: "The God of peace".

Even in the Hindu scriptures, God is peace *(Om shanti shanti, shanti, om)*. It is obvious that God desires His children to live in peace and enjoy the beauty of His creation. It appears that it shall be so in the coming age, as Stephen Gill says in his poem: "Prince of Peace". It seems, he is referring to Millennium or the Age of Truth (*Satyug*) in the Hindu philosophy:

> He shall awaken
> the season of blossoming.
> Prince is
> the strength in the autumn
> that is plagued by wasps.[5]

Stephen Gill expresses a hope. He describes this hope in his novel when he talks of a world government. Hope is there also in several poems. Prof. Dr. Frank Tierney finds that in the poetry of Stephen Gill,

> Although...prevailing tone is cynical of mankind's contemporary attitude, there is hope for those persons and nations who transcend selfishness, aggressiveness and opportunism. There is, in Mr. Gill's mature work, a public despair but private hope. Survival and growth of the person and the nation begins with inner enlightenment, inner awareness of the principle of survival — love... there is in...Mr. Gill's volume a hierarchy of values. The first and most important is, as John Henry Newman insisted, "growth within." This growth requires spiritual priority. This principle leads man to personal, national and international harmony through an understanding that comes from love.[6]

Mr. Pritam Singh also finds this kind of optimistic note in the poetry of Stephen Gill:

> Stephen Gill is more concerned with the sunny side rather than seamy side of life. He takes optimistic view of life. He fixes his gaze at far distant horizon where there is always a rainbow for him. He always strives and longs for a rosy future. "Dreams For Sale" is one of the most representative poems in this mood.[7]

Political, religious and business leaders have perverted the true meaning of pure religion and have turned it into a weapon of mass destruction on the basis of prejudices and lust for money, power, fame, and glory. In order to achieve these symbols of success, humans have turned themselves into beasts – predators, eating alive their victims and leaving behind only death.

A favourite sub-paradox is the movie industry. This sub-paradox represents actors of prominence, who stand against wars and dirty politics. Yet, the same actors play in the movies that are filled with wars, violence, and perversions. The people who stand against wars and violence may not comprehend the fact that most wars in families, neighbourhoods, as well as the greatest percentage of acts of violence are largely due to the fact that there is no control on the film industry.

A devastating product of war is famine. That is what Stephen Gill says, "I rather believe/ famine is man-made/ and sunshine a child of peace."[8] This is still another paradox. According to one estimate 10% of the population of the world controls 90 per cent of the world's finances. This is not fair.

Everything, when not taken care of, degrades and dies, whether it is a non-living object or a living object. Humans do not take care of their bodies, habits, behaviour, and the place where they live and still they want to be healthy and live forever. They spend billions of dollars to recover what humans previously destroyed. This is another paradox!

In the world, there is so much pain, including the pain from rejection, loneliness, pain from not being able to provide for the family, losing a loved one, being powerless against the systems of this world, and the pains due to fear and torments. People would give everything so they can have peace and be acknowledged by others. If somebody wants to be acknowledged, they would lose their inward peace to achieve it. They do not treasure their peace because of their strife to become famous and be widely acknowledged. Those who do not have peace hanker after fame and acknowledgement to have peace, not knowing that they are after a mirage. These desires for peace and acknowledgement also form a paradox.

The following words from *Immigrant, a* novel by Stephen Gill, amplify this way of thinking:

> People in the west seek peace in yoga, meditation and eastern values, whereas easterners envy the westerners, for their hard work and material comforts and in their scientific progress. From time immemorial man has sought peace in various objects and places always ending in despair. A child, the father of man, is an ideal example. He is never satisfied with one toy for long. He keeps changing his pursuits or games. As a grown-up man, he plays with other forms of toys, such as politics, health, money, education, marriage, sex, children; but nothing brings him a lasting happiness. Man seems to be destined for this end. Tolstoy had everything to be proud of. He was awarded the highest degrees and honors that a nation can bestow on its worthy child. He had wealth, good health, his children were obedient and good, yet the poor man continuously sought for peace of mind. He often thought of killing himself.[9]

Stephen Gill explains the same philosophy though in a different way in his poem "Harmony and Peace", where he says, "I searched for you/ within the walls of temples/ mosques and shrines/ in poor man's places/ the mansions of graces...." The poem ends with the following lines:

> For which of those sins
> offences and crimes
> have we lost the time to breathe?
> No hope, no spark
> to own your tranquil eyes.[10]

The message in Stephen Gill's writing is that humans have become proud, selfish, self-consuming and are not concerned about others. This is a way to lose peace and harmony. Humans have to be humble and caring in the image of the Lord who has created everyone to prosper in peace. This is what *Rig Veda*, a Hindu scripture, means when it advises citizens of the world to live in harmony and speak with one voice.[11]

References

1. Stephen Gill, *Shrine* (Arizona: World University Press, 1999), p. 8.
2. Stephen Gill, *Songs Before Shrine* (Delhi: Authorspress, 2007), p.54.

3. Stephen Gill, *Shrine*, p.49.
4. *The Bible* (Old Testament), Judges, 6:24.
5. Stephen Gill, *Songs Before Shrine*, p.109.
6. Frank Tierney, "Reflection of An Indian Poet", *Glimpses*, ed. Hamadan Darwesh (Ontario: Vesta, 2005), p.151.
7. Pritam Singh, "Little Punjab In Canada", *Glimpses*, pp. 45- 46.
8. Stephen Gill, *Shrine*, p.157.
9. Stephen Gill, *Immigrant* (Ontario: Vesta, 1982), p.106.
10. Stephen Gill, *Songs Before Shrine*, p.15.
11. *Rig Veda*, 10: 191: 2-3.

10

Cross-Cultural Conflicts in Stephen Gill's *Immigrant* (1982)

—O.P. Dwivedi

> The history of immigration is the history of alienation and its consequences. For every freedom won, a tradition lost. For every second generation assimilated, a first generation in one way or another spurned. For the gains of goods and services, an identity lost, and uncertainty found.[1]

Immigrant, a thought-provoking novel by Stephen Gill, who is an Indian by birth and who is now settled in Canada, touches on a very real problem, a facet of Kipling's 'East is East, West is West / And ne'er the twain shall meet'. It is a psychological study of the love-hate relationship the immigrants experience in a totally new country and opens a new vista for prospective immigrants leaving behind their native land and settling in Canada. It is the painful experience of the immigrants that I propose to deal with in this paper.

Stephen Gill's duality of vision — a vision being the product of his upbringing in India and his settlement in Canada later on — enables him to discern both the Canadians and Indians on an equal scale of measurement. Like a true, unbiased social activist, Gill takes up the issues of cultural identity and acculturation, oppression and exploitation of the Asian immigrants at the hands of the Whites, a by-product of the cultural difference pointing to the pathetic condition of the immigrants. In this connection, Vijay Misra, a renowned literary critic, states thus: "All diasporas are unhappy, but every diaspora is unhappy in its own way."[2]

Gill's *Immigrant*, states R.K. Singh, "is an exploration in immigrant's aspirations for economic livelihood, social well-being and intercultural understanding *vis-a-vis* the dimensions of the centrality of communication and politics in the affairs of the people."[3] How race and culture restrict and haunt one's life in a foreign country can be seen in the unhappy experiences of Reghu Nath, the protagonist of the novel. Racial prejudice and threat to the native's job are the two reasons for germinating the seeds of distrust and hatred. Almost the entire postcolonial literature is the outcome of these distressing attitudes.

Of late, the concept of the immigrant has undergone a severe change. Earlier, one used to undertake a journey to a foreign country mostly for education, and once the education was finished one returned home. But nowadays one goes to a foreign country for education and economic upliftment. When one gets better prospects, one settles in that country, to the embarrassment of the Whites. After ruling over the Orientals for such a long time, such an attitude of the Whites is bound to arise. In his novel, *Immigrant*, Gill creates "a text and a context to cope with the politics of sharing and survival, the communication problems and socio-economic and political contradictions, ambiguities and racist and ethnic prejudices that cause disillusionment and distrust in an immigrant in everyday life."[4] The issue of survival continuously receives a dent in the novel. Prabha, a graduate in Library Science, commits suicide in the stifling atmosphere around.

Immigrant revolves round the central figure of Reghu Nath, whose sufferings and harrowing experiences in Canada constitute the crux of the novel. The novel opens with Reghu Nath flying from India over the Atlantic and landing in Montreal (Canada). Fear begins to grip him as soon as he lands in Canada, as the plane is late by seven hours and this makes him anxious about his registration at the University of Ottawa. But this is just the beginning of his long and anguished stay in Canada. His desire to obtain a Ph.D. from the Ottawa University is further complicated by the communication barrier caused by his unfamiliarity with the Canadian accent. Unlike the other White colleagues, he is made to work hard without getting any appreciation. At the university, he "found himself in a mess because he didn't know the number or type of courses he was to take."[5] Contemptuous of the professors' attitude, Reghu decides to quit the University without obtaining the long-cherished degree.

Reghu's lack of knowledge about the Canadian culture and society comes to the fore when while shopping he holds the hands of a compatriot unaware of the fact that such an act would present them as 'homos'. He is left wondering how holding one's hand can change his identity. Henceforth, he observes the Canadian people closely practising hybridity, a quality found so commonly among the Orients, being unaware of the fact that the cultural vacuum can be hardly filled up in a country suffering from the loss of identity and individuality.

Reghu definitely suffers from a sense of isolation and nostalgia for the homeland. Being new to a foreign land, he fails to find a nice friend with whom he can share his secrets and experiences. His friendship with Akram, an ex-professor at the Karachi University, is only a momentary one, and his sudden encounter with one of his neighbours, who is pursuing a music course in the University of New York, enhances his inferiority complex — a state of mind so formed due to the civilising mission of the Whites. The obvious result is:

> Reghu went up to the apartment when the musician invited him. Unexpectedly, Reghu met with an unusual welcome. The man pulled out an empty beer bottle from under the bed and asked Reghu to return it and buy a beer for him. (40)

These painful experiences sometimes provoke him to go back to India, but he quickly reverts realising that such an act would make him a subject of mockery among his friends and relatives, and moreover he does not have enough money to undertake a return journey. He realises the fact that his past life was now an illusion and the present situation was the hardcore reality, hence he opts to live in the present and in such a situation, he proclaims: "The whole world is my country. I am a world citizen" (42) thus dismissing, in one stroke the very Western concept of nations, and spreading the unheard message of universal peace and brotherhood. To talk of world citizenship is easier said than done especially at such a time when the concept of nation is proliferating across the globe; nevertheless Gill must be congratulated for his noble concept of world citizenship.

Reghu seems to be a young man deeply influenced by movies; that is why in his very first meeting with an unknown girl he "mustered all his courage to say politely 'I love you'. The girl glanced to oneside, then the other, before finishing her whisky in a gulp" (p.10). But the girl does not respond, leaving him completely dozed and baffled. Once more, his native culture gets a shock:

> Women in Canada do not expect to hear the words 'I love you' at the first meeting. It sounds phony to them – after all, they have to know the man first (21).

Gill seems to be contemptuous of the parents' role in India in fixing the marriages of their sons and daughters. He makes us see that marriage in India is not a bond between a boy and a girl, but it is a mutual settlement between two families.

Failing to find any girlfriend, Reghu tries his tricks on Mrs. Wallace, a freelance writer of sixty, to satisfy his physical needs. He is successful in taking her to bed, but the skeleton-like figure of Mrs. Wallace cools down the fire of his lust. Henceforth he has a series of short-lived affairs with the white girls, but they turn out to be bitter ones. He now realises that "the white girls expect to be treated as special, almost as China dolls, and disliked being touched in any way on the first date" (22), and further "A woman has to be emotionally involved with a man before she gives herself to him."(24)

Reghu thus learns a hard lesson about the Western culture, and his frustration seems to grow much and more. All his frustration reminds of what Salman Rushdie stated in his popular novel, *Shame* (1983):

> What is the best thing about migrant people...? I think it is their hopefulness.... And what's the worst thing? It's the emptiness of one's luggage.... We've come unstuck from more than land. We've floated upwards from history, from memory, from time.[6]

Rushdie thus tries to clear the presuppositions of the immigrants, highlighting their problems related to nations and identity.

Gill sometimes seems to be highly critical of the degrading moral values in the West. Mrs. Clifford, a woman in her late fifties is a paradigm of this assertion. She says:

> I love people from the East. They're polite, wise and nonaggressive. I wish I were an Eastern mother! (100)

And further she says:

> We've lost our feelings and sentiments, and have become as cold as our snow. Socially we're dead... we no longer have blood in our veins. (101).

Mrs. Clifford is a widow and her son has left her alone in pursuit of his business. Gill takes up her issue and highlights the painful condition that the old people face in Canada. He frowns on the dying human values just for the sake of money. The loneliness of the Westerns in their old age once again presents the stern reality that every aged person needs someone to support him/her in old age. This reality is rapidly spreading everywhere in the human world. Apparently, the self-assertion of the youths is the real cause for this malady.

Racial incidents pervade the novel throughout. The novelist remarks: "A youth was slapped and pushed by white boys from the Toronto Station platform on the subway track..." (116-117). As a result, the young man suffers severe injuries and is admitted in a hospital for almost eight months. Many schools in Toronto do not allow the Asian students to study some particular subjects. An Asian in Toronto is harassed by a child and ironically he is fined two-hundred dollars for hitting back the child slightly. In another biased action of the police, when a white man hits a car of an Asian and accepts his fault, the police does not take any appropriate action. Reghu himself becomes a victim of the police's partial actions for hitting a pick-up van while trying to flee away from the intimidating truck-driver who is quite content to turn him blue-black. He is fined eighty dollars by the cruel and callous police, paying no attention to the rude behaviour of the truck-driver. These incidents fracture the hopes of the immigrants, overcrowding Canada. They are treated as a cancer. This bitter truth of racism also haunts Bharti Mukherjee, a famous Indian novelist, now an immigrant to America, who in an interview with Alison B. Carb confesses:

> The seventies were horrendous for Indians in Canada. There was lot of bigotry against Canadian citizens of Indian origin, especially in Toronto....Toronto made me a civil rights activist. I wrote about devastating personal effects of racism....[6]

Taking note of Uma Parameswaran's famous quote, "Home is where the feet are, and we had better place our heart where the feet are," [7] Reghu adopts the Canadian citizenship, which doesn't fetch any relief to his woes. He still remains jobless and runs from hand to mouth situation throughout. Reghu should have realised that the question is not about citizenship but about the colour of his skin. Subsequently, Gill talks about the need to understand one's culture. Speaking of the importance of 'culture (-s)', a renowned analyst of Freudian studies states thus:

> Cultures have the same properties as the individual personality in that they possess nuclear and peripheral areas of organisation, and we might picture each culture(culture is to society what personality is to individual) as a huge jigsaw puzzle with its center composed of closely fitted interlocked pieces while nearer the periphery lie more loosely-organised pieces and even pieces which are not interlocked at all.[8]

Clearly, the cultural constraints determine the behaviour – actions and reactions — of the individual in a given society.

To conclude, Stephen Gill as an expatriate writer tries to clear the false preconceived notions of the Asian immigrants. He sends a crystal-clear message to the third-world people who are quite keen on entering into the first-world with strong aspirations for a better future without realizing that this displacement to the first-world demands greater adaptability in terms of both climate and culture.

References

1. http://www.brocku.ca/english/courses/1F95/Immigrant.html
2. Vijay Misra, *The Literature of the Indian Diaspora: Theorising The Diasporic Imaginary* (London: Routledge, 2007), p.1.
3. R.K. Singh, "Cross-Cultural Communication", *Language Forum* Vol. XXIV, Nos. 1- 2, p.2.
4. Ibid.
5. Stephen Gill, *Immigrant* (Ontario: Vesta, 1982), p.16. All subsequent references to this novel are absorbed in the paper itself.
6. Cited from Jasbir Jain's *Writers of the Indian Diaspora* (Jaipur: Rawat Publications, 2003), p.58.
7. Uma Parameswaran, "Home is where your feet are, and may your heart be there too!", ed. *Writers of the Indian Diaspora*, p.39.
8. J.A.C. Brown, *Freud and Post-Freudians* (Harmondsworth: Penguin Books, 1964), p.121.

11

Angst of Alienation in Stephen Gill's Poetry

—*Shweta Saxena*

Stephen Gill's poetry is conspicuous for its message of peace and harmony in the society. Through his poems, he affirms his belief that "the malady of religious and racial fanaticism and violence lies in the acceptance of the values of tolerance, understanding, and co-existence" (*Shrine* 26). Besides this, his poetry contains abiding echoes of an alienated artistic soul. The present paper tries to foreground flashes of existential *angst* that lie dormant in the poetry of Gill. The *angst* of alienation, which is felt very often by an artistic soul, can influence a person in two ways—in a negative way it can make him a pessimist and escapist, while acting positively, it can motivate a person to work more vigorously towards making this world a better place. Accordingly, the present paper endeavours to reveal that in Stephen Gill's poetry the *angst* of alienation was experienced as a positive force that impelled him to become a committed artist, striving for the cause of betterment of humanity.

Sifting through the pages of Gill's poetry collections, it is not difficult to find the agony of an isolated soul. This alienation and isolation might have sprung from the fact that he witnessed from close quarters the fury of religious fanaticism and the agony of displacement, both physical and mental. C. L. Khatri recommends that "his poetry should be read and evaluated in the light of his past nightmarish experiences in India when communal riots broke out in the wake of partition of India. It made him migrate from India and settle in Canada. But there also the memories of brutality and tortured childhood always kept haunting him like his own shadow. Purged in the fire of sufferings the young Stephen evolved into a muse full of compassion and he made it a summum bonum of his life to fight the violence, hatred and enmity and embrace the suffering masses with love and sympathy" (188). His poetry collection *Shrine* abounds with the images of a lonely and desolated soul that passionately aspires to break the obdurate mould of racial and communal orthodoxy and liberate humanity from its hold. In the poem titled "Self", Gill acknowledges himself as "A homeless beggar" who wanders "to catch a glimpse of reality/from different angles/on the pieces of glass" (45). Again in the poem "An Immigrant Complains", he voices out the despair of a lonely soul:

> His feathers flutter
> wounded by sickles of bigotry
> in an estranged world
> around the isle of loneliness. (78)

Here Gill sounds very much like the existentialist philosopher Kierkegaard, who stands "like a lonely fir tree, egotistically isolated, looking toward something higher, . . . throwing no shadow, only the wood dove building its nest in [his] branches" (qtd. in Jaspers 177). Further in the poem "Legacy", Gill says that he has planted in his yard "the trees/ which give the fruits of pain/fear, loneliness/and self-destruction" (93).

But the poet does not want his progeny to bear this pain, hence he wishes to leave "abundant pills" of peace and harmony to relieve his children from the "headache" of animosity. These pills are nothing but his poems that are filled with the profoundest emotion of amity. In order to soothe his disturbed psyche, he moves from place to place, but his terrible thoughts refuse to leave his company. In the poem "Tenants in Me", he admits that even after immigrating to a peaceful land, he is unable to forget the horror of inhuman violence in the name of religion that inflicted the place of his birth:

> The immigrant in me
> talks of the days
> when religiosity killed innocents
> of different creeds.
>
> Those painful shrieks
> hidden in his blood
> stagger at night. (153)

Gill professes in the poem "A New Canadian in Toronto" that even in the city of Toronto he does not find peace, since "the lips of this city/ smell like the plastic flowers/and its eyes display/the festivals of the orphans" (141). He feels isolated in the city of Toronto, for "the word friendship/you'll hardly find in its book. /The cover is attractive though/ there is nothing inside to read. /The words are hieroglyphic; /it needs ages to decipher them" (141). The pang that reflects through these lines is the one felt by an "immigrant who has lived through and survived against the hostility generated mainly out of the uncosmopolitan profile of his so-called cosmopolitan surroundings. The range of emotions and sentiments experienced by Gill is common to most of the unfairly treated immigrants. The supercilious attitude of the mainstream citizens, hurtful insults and motivated racial assaults cripple them both physically and psychologically and, as a reaction to the feeling of hurt, they take recourse in voicing their protest through the medium of writing" (Singh and Sarkar 171).

Gill's poetry collection *Songs Before Shrine* vividly conveys the alienation and isolation felt by an artist. In the poem "Birth of Poems" he writes:

> Poets free
> the birds of their blood
> and
> weave purrs and growls
> with a single loom.
> They are cats
> walking in the darkness of solitude. (32)

In another poem "Isle of Art", the poet paints the picture of an isolated island that provides him peace and comfort, and serves as a retreat "from the life-stifling smoke/from the heartbreak house" (37). Further in the poem "The World of Poetry", he writes:

> The world of poetry
> is woven with rainbow strings
> sorted in the secret caves of desire
> to recreate
> the source of that supreme grace
> that evolves
> in the womb of solitary hours
> during the creative nights of its
> conception. (40)

However, the desire for peace and solitude, expressed in these lines, seems to be a prerequisite for artistic creation. It should not be seen as one with the kind of social alienation expressed elsewhere in Gill's poetry.

The recurring voices of alienation suggest a deep rooted existential *angst* in the psyche of the poet. In the existential philosophy there are two distinguishing "stages of *Angst*. In the first instance, *Angst* is the disturbing and 'uncanny' mood which summons a person to reflect on his individual existence and its 'possibilities'. It is this which people are more than ready to pass off as a 'funny turn', returning with relief to the 'tranquillising' ways of the 'they'. But suppose a person 'faces up' to his *Angst*, accepting the truths about his existence which it intimates. Then a number of options appear, including modulation into that resolute, sober and 'joyful' *Angst* to which Heidegger refers" (Cooper 128). In Gill's poetry these two successive stages of *Angst* are clearly discernible.

In the poem "Me", the poet thoughtfully reflects over the possibilities of his own existence and writes, "I want to ask/how I am/ Let me find me/my smiles/my own hurts" (30). The poem titled "Self" also contains an enquiry after the true nature of the poet's existence, wherein he tries to seek his original self by peeping into the mirror of psyche, surveying the landscapes of books, looking into the lakes of strange eyes, swimming across the waters of solitude, roaming in the jungles of thoughts and exploring mirages (44). After coming face to face with the disturbing reality, the poet, however, does not pass it off as a 'funny turn', he rather faces up to it. Since "the kind of nirvana he contemplates comes neither from renouncing the world nor sitting before the idols of gods and chanting their names but in establishing a harmonious social order" (Chambial 167). The existential *Angst* positively motivates him to strive for such "forms of thought and existence in which people are 'at home' with their world and each other, but not at the cost of 'losing themselves'" (Cooper 33). Gill's anxiety is rooted in his desire for making this world a better place, for which he incessantly strives in his poetry. Maryanne Raphael rightly describes his poetry and writes, "his poems are strong and yet tender, mysterious at times; at others, comfortable and comforting, like old slippers to be worn around the house. But he does not allow us to relax for long, for suddenly there is a scorpion of a metaphor ready to shock us into an awareness necessary for our psychological and spiritual growth. Stephen's poetry penetrates our most private perceptions. No matter how unthreatening and restful it may appear, there is always a surprise to jolt us forward, much like the power of a koan" (155).

Gill seeks to ward off the ghost of alienation by escaping, very often, in the peaceful world of the dove, which is a recurring image in his poetry. In the poem "To a Dove", he says that "enveloped by my own shadows/I dare to enter your brave world/of rainbow colours/which nourish your flowing life" (144). In another poem "Flight of the Dove", he depicts the world of dove as unblemished from the faults of human beings:

> I hear
> some unknown voice calling her
> to be above the confusing cries
> of mindless feverishness
> and the hounds of alienation
> from the houses of infamy
> of social upheavals. (145)

In fact the image of 'dove' emerges rather prominently in Gill's poetry and it is pregnant with some deep meaning and significance. Explaining the symbolic significance of 'dove' in different religions and cultures, he states: "the name dove is given to a bird in the pigeon family. Doves live throughout the world from deserts to tropical forests. Due to its soft cooing sound and affectionate disposition it is symbolised as the emblem of peace. Among Christians, it is used for God's love in any manifestation. In Christian art it often symbolises hope, peace, Holy Spirit and even martyrdom. The dove also signifies the soul as well as gentleness and purity" (Sarangi 4). In Gill's poetry also 'dove' carries different connotations at different places. Sometimes it is symbolic of peace, other times of poetic imagination, and at still other it signifies divine grace. The imagery of 'dove', in all its varied manifestations, appears to be suggesting cure for the alienated soul of the poet and encouraging him on the path of attaining a fuller existence.

Another significant aspect of Gill's poetry is that the alienation of the poet is not a self-inflicted exile; it is due to the circumstances of his being that he finds himself aloof from the general current of humanity. The sense of seclusion naturally gives a melancholic tone to his poetry. In R. K. Singh's opinion, "the overall atmosphere created in the poems reflecting his sociopolitical awareness is one of gloom and despair with a degree of pronounced melancholia. Disappointment is the keynote of this melancholia, whether with edgy complications of social insecurity or with insoluble problems of political instability" (172). But deep in his heart there is also a desire to assimilate in the mainstream of life. Praising Gill for spreading the message of mutual love and tolerance Rochelle L. Holt writes, "while most are struggling in the Nineties to stress the differences of many cultures, Stephen Gill is professing the opposite, a more complex cognition which the masses have not yet learned in yearning for separate glorification of each race, each colour, each sex, each age. . . . the poet tells us through his work that we are beyond brotherhood and sisterhood as we achieve the forgotten meaning of 'neighbourhood', not isolated and separate but one large melting pot where we all appreciate our uniqueness while affirming our similarities" (160). In the poem "Go Back", Gill asserts that he considers himself an inseparable part of the country of his migration, that is, Canada:

> I came here
> carrying the lily of my dreams.
> I have offered
> the boon of my life
> to my new mother
> and the warmth of my blood
> to the snow. (80)

Gill expresses his full faith in the notion of universal brotherhood and appeals to his detractor that he should give up his parochialism, since "the world has become a village/where no one is an island to self/ anymore/anymore" (82). In his poem "My Canada" from the collection *Songs Before Shrine*, Gill praises Canada for its multicultural ethos:

> Thy soul
> a serene temple
> for every creed
> for every breed.
> My heart will sing
> always for thee
> my lips will chant
> night and day for thee
> O Canada. (21)

Gill feels that in Canada there are ample opportunities for an artist to work freely. And like Sartre, Gill also perceives his freedom in being a part of the society at large, not in egotistical detachment. In Sartre's view, "freedom is discovered only in the act, is one with the act; it is the foundation of the connections and interactions which constitute the internal structure of the act; it never is enjoyed but is revealed in and by its products; it is not an inner power of snatching one's self out of the most urgent situations, for there is no outside or inside for man. But it exists, on the contrary, for engaging one's self in present action and constructing a future, it is that by which there is born a future which permits understanding and changing the present" (qtd. in Grene 7-8). In Gill's opinion poets should exercise their creative power to influence the society, he states that the "poets are involved with many aspects of life . . . . Lorca and Byron gave their lives for the cause of liberation. Among the written documents, *the Vedas, the Bible,* and *the Koran* have a great impact on the minds of people. Lately, Pentagon papers concerning the Vietnam War have changed the thinking of several Americans, and a book titled *Uncle Tom's Cabin* by Harriet Beecher Stow was partly responsible for the liberation of the slaves in the USA. I hope that my writings about peace will cause change in the thinking of my readers" (Agarwal 4-5).

Gill's poetic vision aspires to change the unfortunate condition of the present by envisaging a glorious future full of "unconditional love and global peace through a democratically elected world government" (Gill, *Shrine* 26). Ultimately, he believes in the life of action, not of renouncement. He is self-avowedly a committed poet, who wishes to convey the message of harmonious co-existence to the strife-torn humanity and soothe its bruised soul. Thus the *Angst* of alienation in Gill's poetry acts as a catalyst in catapulting him on his journey in search of a meaningful and spiritually fulfilling existence.

Works Cited

Agarwal,N.K. "Stephen Gill on His Writing and Diaspora", *Asian Tribune*.August13,2007.Oct10,2007.<http://www.asiantribune.com/index.php?q=node/6943>.

Chambial, D. C. "Songs for Harmony", 1999. *Glimpses*. Ed. Hamadan Darwesh. Cornwall: Vesta, 2005. 167-68.

Cooper, David E. *Existentialism*. Oxford: Blackwell, 1992.

Gill, Stephen. *Shrine*. Benson: World University Press, 1999.

________________. *Songs Before Shrine*. New Delhi: Authorspress, 2007.

Grene, Marjorie. *Introduction to Existentialism*. Chicago: University of Chicago Press, 1968.

Holt, Rochelle L. "A Call for Peace." 1992. *Glimpses*. Ed. Hamadan Darwesh. Cornwall: Vesta, 2005. 157-60.

Jaspers, Karl. "Existenzphilosophie", *Existentialism from_Dostoevsky to Sartre.* Ed.Walter Kaufmann. Cleveland: World Publishing Company, 1962. 131-205.

Khatri,C.L. Rev. of *Shrine* by Stephen Gill. 1999. *Glimpses.* 186-87.

Raphael, Maryanne. "Gill's Poetry Enriches Our Life." 1998. *Glimpses.* 154-56.

Sarangi, Jaydeep. Interview with Stephen Gill. *Pakistan Christian Post.* 4th Sep, 2007. Oct 2, 2007. <http://www.pakistanchristianpost.com/newsdetails.php?newsid=544>.

Singh, R. K. and Mitali De Sarkar. "A Search for Elysium", 1998. *Glimpses.* 169-81.

12

A Critique of Stephen Gill's Literary Sensibility

—Nilanshu Kumar Agarwal

> Things fall apart; the centre cannot hold;
> Mere anarchy is loosed upon the world,
> The blood dimmed tide is loosed, and everywhere
> The ceremony of innocence is drowned;
> The best lack all conviction, while the worst
> Are full of passionate intensity. (Yeats, 211).

A reading of the aforesaid lines makes us believe that Yeats reached the nadir of despair in "The Second Coming". Yeats is disturbed by the contemporary sordid and degraded society. Through the portrayal of this spiritual miasma in "The Second Coming", Yeats seems to signify that there exists an ethical void in the modern world. The same mood of inner anguish and despair is also perceptible in the literary works of Stephen Gill, the poet laureate of Ansted University. A note of feverish anxiety runs through all his works. It is worthwhile to say that this deadening sense of pathetic grief is due to his own previous experiences. In the Preface to *Shrine,* Gill has emotionally written about his tragic encounters with stark reality during the post-partition days in India:

> Every time there was a stir caused by the wind, a car on the street, the bark of a dog, or the mew of a cat, we froze inside our house. Every time there was anything unusual, unseen tragedy was expected. The nights were nightmares and the days did not bring any hope. Often the mornings dawned with more lamentable events. It was not easy to sleep when night after night the ghosts of fear looked straight into our eyes. It turned into

> an obsession that afflicted me every minute of every hour that whom to trust and to take in confidence. Passers-by and neighbours appeared to be the possible killers. Apparently to me, the dragons of religious terror for minorities roamed around freely. (8-9)

This sense of damned insecurity created emotional stir in the man and the result is the invaluable literary output. It is an established fact that certain emotional experiences create a unique type of poetic upsurge in the poet's heart; poetry blooms when a typical emotion disturbs the sensitive psyche of the creative artist. In Wordsworth's view too, "poetry is the spontaneous overflow of powerful feelings." Satya Dev Choudhary has dwelt in great detail on this process of poetic creation:

> ...when a poet through any source, becomes familiar with any object or incident—and also some time becomes emotionally involved with it—it gets imprinted in his mind. And it, at some occasion with the aid of his imaginative faculty, bursts out spontaneously in multi forms of expression. This very expression is called a fine piece of poetic work—whether in versification or in prose. (216)

Satya Dev Choudhary adds:

> The forceful influence of any object or event on the mind of the poet is transferred into an appropriate expression with the help of his imagination. (217)

The partition fury filled the heart of Gill with compassion and pity for the humanity and it resulted in the creation of works like *Shrine* and *Songs Before Shrine*, where his mission is to bring peace to the world. About this poetic process Gill had told me in an interview:

> Poetry is a spiritual and psychic experience. To give shape to this experience, poets need special knowledge in order to use images, tones, economy of words and other techniques. To weave a rainbow of beauty, poets select and adjust words in different combinations.

This moulding of Gill's poetic voice out of an emotional experience is somewhat akin to sage Valmiki's transformation into an epic poet. About Valmiki's metamorphosis, G.B.Mohan eloquently writes:

> The poet transmutes his experience into a rhythmic verbal pattern of sensuous images and dynamic characters and the reader, in his turn, translates the pattern into a relishable experience... The legend about the incident which occasioned the composition of the epic *Ramayana* is instructive. When the sage Valmiki saw one of the *Krauñca* pair shot dead by a hunter, he was overcome by sorrow. But his sorrow was transformed into infinite compassion for human suffering. This was an occasion for his creative imagination to start conjuring up forms, images and characters. His heart overflowed with creative compassion which was different from his personal sorrow. The creative experience occasioned by the contemplation of the sorrowful incident issued forth in the epic *Ramayana*.... Unless the poet himself is suffused with rasa, he can not infuse it into his work. It is evident that this rasa of the poet, which is a contemplative creative experience and not a personal emotion, is the root of all poetic process. (10)

Mulk Raj Anand has also written thus about Valmiki's catalysis:

> The story is related that Valmiki was out one day gathering sacrificial wood and grass in the forest when he saw a pair of *Krauñca* birds joyfully twittering as they sat on the branch of a tree. An arrow came that very instant from an invisible hunter and struck the male bird, which instantly fell. The sage was filled with immense grief to reflect that only a moment ago the poor creature was happily singing, and now it lay dead in the dust, while its companion fluttered about it shrieking with anguish. Long did the incident trouble Valmiki's mind that day, and the poignant tragedy lay heavy on his heart till he burst out in an ecstatic verse of exquisite melody and pathos, and became lost in the forgetfulness of pure bliss. (385)

So, the personal experiences of a poet create his poetic voice. Eliot has also spoken of the necessity of personal emotions for the true poetic effluence, while discussing the two types of impersonality. In his essay on W.B.Yeats, Eliot writes:

> There are two forms of impersonality: that which is natural to the mere skilful craftsman, and which is more and more achieved by the maturing artist. The first is that of what I have called 'the anthology piece' of a lyric by Lovclace or Suckling, or of Campion... The second impersonality is that of the poet, who out of intense and personal experience, is able to express a general truth: retaining all the particularities of his experience to make of it a general symbol. (189)

To be short, certain experiences leave the indelible imprint on the psyche of the poet and in his creative works, he universalises that particular personal emotion. Stephen Gill has done the same thing by universalising his traumatic partition experiences. The harrowing tale of partition riot is eloquently painted by Gill in the following manner:

> During these riots, we did not know if there would be another dawn and when there was, it brought tales of more brutalities. I saw old people running for help and being pelted with bricks and then burnt alive while the patrolling police ignored the clusters of misguided zealots who were in the street in spite of curfews. I perceived death dancing in the eyes of minorities, heard the cries of infants .and read about the butchery of the innocent as if that was happening in front of my eyes (Gill, *Songs Before Shrine*, x-xi).

Here, it is pertinent to remark that Gill is not the only creative artist, who has spoken emotionally about the partition violence. There are authors like Khushwant Singh and Manohar Malgonkar, who have written about partition horrors that haunted India and Pakistan. Shyamala A. Narayan and John Mee have called Khushwant Singh's *Train To Pakistan* "the best regarded novel in English about partition". (220) William Walsh has written thus about the treatment of partition fury in this novel:

> The objectivity, detachment and impartiality of *Train to Pakistan* make the horrors it describes—a train standing in the station with Sikh corpses from Pakistan, another packed with Muslims massacred in India—with all their madness and ferocity all the more convincing, all the more devastating. (99)

In a way, this soul-stirring novel presents a realistic portrait of the bestial horrors, which swept the subcontinent during that chaotic time. The novel, presenting a pathetic tale of a Punjab village called Mano-Majra, leaves an impression of the basic animal like cruelty of the man on the reader's mind. V.A.Shahane has written thus about *Train To Pakistan*:

> It is a grim story of individuals and communities caught up in the vortex of the partition of undivided India into two states in 1947. (345)

Manohar Malgonkar's *A Bend in The Ganges* presents the same feverish strife, caused by one of the bloodiest upheavals of the contemporary history. K.R.S.Iyengar in his seminal book *Indian Writing in English* has written thus about the novel:

> *A Bend in The Ganges* is an attempt to unfold this national tragedy....No doubt it needs Tolstoy, if not Vyasa, to tell the whole unvarnished story of united India breaking up into two, experiencing the terrific convulsions of unimaginable fratricidal strife. (432)

Like these two masters of Indian English fiction, Stephen Gill is also in deep anguish on account of the blood dimmed tide of partition. To borrow an expression from Hardy, during those days, "ancient pulse of germ and birth/ Was shrunken hard and dry." What Hardy had said about the close of the nineteenth century, is also true about India and Pakistan of partition days. The following discussion by Gill about the victims of partition in "Author's Preface" to *Shrine* is sure to touch the innermost chords of the reader's heart:

> I cannot forget the climate of New Delhi which emitted a strong offensive smell due to the rotting dead bodies in the houses. It was said that the government had their buses loaded with bodies to be burnt somewhere outside the city. The authorities could not find adequate loaders because of the stench. Even the water became polluted because several dead bodies were thrown into the Yamuna River which was the source of supply for the city residents. (11)

'The weariness, the fever and the fret' caused by the naked fury of the partition violence made him sing in full-throated ease the sickening agonies of the refugees, as is clear from the following lines:

> A smoke of uncertainty
> surrounds them like fear
> and the albatross of loneliness
> sits upon them
> like a paperweight.
> They need every moment
> someone to share
> the stale banquet of the past:
> a ghost
> for them that is still real. (Gill, *Shrine*, 76-77)

As is common with any literary genius, Gill has universalised his personal anguish; because of his first hand experience of the human predicament during the partition riots, he has a typical emotional bond with the suffering humanity. For example, the poet has deep sympathies for the people of Somalia, overshadowed by 'the tribal smoke of animosity'. In the poem "Somali Victim of 1992 Tribal Warfare", Gill is crying for "the man-made lake of starvation":

> Around him lay
> emaciated rag-clothed kids.
> Some have swollen bellies
> and some sores on their heads,
> hands or feet.
> They carry scabies.
> Rashes, fever, malaria are common;
> medicine is scarce. (Gill, *Shrine*, 74)

In the same poem, the following lines exhibit the curse of starvation in Africa:

> On the shoulder of a mother
> he sees a dozing child,
> ribs staring through flesh.
> Eyelids hardly open,
> are covered with flies.
> They have eaten
> the leaf of the thorn tree;
> now the tree has nothing
> but thorns. (Gill, *Shrine*, 74)

The tragic predicament of the kids during the period of rampant anarchy would have made Wordsworth cry for their lot. Wordsworth had addressed the child as 'thou best philosopher', 'thou Eye among the blind', 'mighty prophet' and 'Seer blest'. That mighty prophet of Wordsworth has 'ribs staring through flesh' in Gill's poetry. Gill's treatment of the starving children fills the reader's heart with 'leaden-eyed despairs' and gloomy anguish.

On account of his humanitarian outlook and moral bent of mind, Gill has presented the poor fate of the common folk in several poems. For example, the following expression from "A Familiar Scene" is sure to wring tears from the eyes of the readers:

> Here is a mother
> who moves the corpses
> to find her son;
> here is the cry of an old man

buried in the cries of the wounded.
Who are these innocents
whom the storm of cruelty
has extinguished
as if they were candles. (Gill, *Shrine*, 69)

Due to experiencing the holocaust of violence during the partition days, his heart is full of pity for the wounded civilisation. In fact, the pain experienced during those days is responsible for his creative urge. In the Preface to *Songs Before Shrine,* he confesses:

> It is the pain of these wounds of life in India that I carry with me no matter where I go....that pain is still alive in the caves of my arteries and comes to life as specters particularly when it is night. The more I try to escape those specters, the more they torment me. That is also my well from where I have and even now I draw the waters of my inspiration. I find that well inexhaustible and its waters more satisfying with every visit to it. These visits are like that of a child to its mother. I carry the luggage of my discomforting experiences wherever I go. (xvi)

In his poem "A Portrait of Today", the realism of Gill is evident, when he depicts the terrible phenomenon:

A harvest of artillery
clouds the journey of peace,
engulfing the roof of human security. (Gill, *Shrine*, 91)

An offshoot of the partition violence is the religious obscurantism, which finds a high emotional treatment in Gill's poetry. In the Preface to *Songs Before Shrine*, he has declared:

> Religious mania produces a fire that would continue burning innocent people....That fire has not solved any problem. When used for political ends, this fire causes untold devastation. It causes untold devastation also when innocent citizens, including infants and normal housewives become fodder to satisfy the hunger of the maniacs.... (xix)

The feverish strife caused by this religious fanaticism has been condemned by Gill in the harshest possible words. For example, mark the following expression from "Religious Fanaticism":

It leads
the adders of dread
destruction
disdain
and distaste. (Gill, *Shrine*, 63)

As a result of this obnoxious religious intolerance, "the time is out of joint" and Gill's denunciation of the beast called man sometimes assumes Swiftian tones. In the manner of the great eighteenth century satirist, the poet anatomises the ugly social scene in "A Familiar Scene":

Bodies rotting in ditches
or dumped with the garbage.
Bodies washing up
onto the beaches
like bundles of clothes
or lying discarded
in open mass graves
heaped together
in grotesque piles. (Gill, *Shrine,* 68)

The frenzy of religious violence has forced the poet to believe that this world is not a fit place to live. 'The plague of intolerance' has choked the beauty of the world. In the poem "Supplication to God", the poet is reporting the debasement of the earth to Him. The man, having 'higher level of intelligence' has devastated the grace of the universe. The poet poetically paints this scenario:

How sweet melodies are repressed
by the strings of overmastering terror.
The pleasing orchard of grace
inhales
the toxin of gunpowder. (Gill, *Songs Before Shrine*, 7)

The condemnation of religious fanaticism by Gill in his works is somewhat similar to Amrinder's *Lajo* and Taslima Nasrin's *Lajja*. While *Lajo* deals with the turbulent periods of 1984 after Mrs. Indira Gandhi's murder; *Lajja* artistically presents the catastrophic India after the demolition of Babri Mosque at Ayodhya. Comparing these two novels, Tapiti Lahiri writes:

A close perusal of the novels testifies to the fact that both Amrinder and Taslima are of the opinion that fundamentalism is

> a disease, a social evil....The political life of the nation can be made strong and healthy and peace can be maintained throughout, if the secular outlook is cultivated in the true sense.... we find that the two writers have gone deep into the malaise from which our whole sub-continent has been suffering, particularly from the day it was partitioned principally on the basis of different religions. (100)

What Tapiti Lahiri had said about these two novels is also true about Gill's poetry, he is internally broken due to this social disease pervading the world in general and the subcontinent in particular.

Due to this depiction of abysmal sense of chaos in the universe, Gill's poetry abounds in certain symbols and images which convey his emotional anger at the unrestrained ferocity of "cold blooded forces/ covered with the skin of fanaticism". The image of the reptiles is very frequent in his verse. In the poem "Humanity", reptiles have assumed human shape:

> Reptiles roam in human form
> on the barren mountain
> of pride
> carrying the flag of their empire
> of evil. (Gill, *Songs Before Shrine*, 57)

Similarly in "Reptiles", venomous snakes of racial discord have crowded his artistic soul. Because of 'the toxin of hate' and 'ulcers of anarchy', spread by these snakes of racial disharmony, the poet's mind and fancy have the numberless images of these reptiles. In 'the mist of fancy', these reptiles have left an indelible impression:

> The serpents of racism
> form images here in the mist of fancy,
> spreading the toxin of hate
> to feed the ulcers of anarchy. (*Songs Before Shrine*, 59).

In one of his haiku poems too, the image of a serpent is repeated:

> Is it rampant reign of humankind
> or the serpent within
> that vomits the lava of hostility? (Gill, *Flashes*, 30).

In the poem "To Humanists", while bewailing the loss of humanity even in the midst of poets and writers, the poet again uses the image of serpent:

> I saw her breathing her last
> in the gatherings of poets
> and writers
> who
> in a frenzy to swallow the sputum
> of their selfish serpent
> ignore exiled artists. (Gill, *Shrine*, 88).

Another important image in his poetry is the image of war. Through this artistic image, Gill has denounced the horrors of the war in the harshest possible terms. In the poem "The Gulf Crisis on TV", he realistically projects the images of 'the Patriots intercepting the Scuds', 'the showers of bullets' and 'the bombs piercing through homes'. Similarly in "Hounds of War", the poet is sorry because the spectre of war has devastated the harmony and peace in the world:

> When
> the hounds of war
> ravage the bridge of harmony
> the melodies of the dove
> die under the leaves
> of slumbering dreams. (Gill, *Shrine*, 56).

In the same vein, the poem "Convictions" has a number of war images like 'language of weapons', 'the daggers of hunger', 'ditches of gold', 'bombs', 'spectres of misery' and 'lips of the sword' etc.

Through these realistic images and symbols, Gill is able to construct a universe of 'famished walking skeletons', 'forlorn infants', 'mute messages of the eyes', 'atrocities never told' and 'souls of the wounded'. In a way, he is a social realist, who has presented a true picture of the 'gloomy pages of life'. Due to his social concern, the poet in the poem "Year After Year" is disturbed by the fact that the common humanity suffers from 'heavy taxes', 'higher unemployment', 'soaring prices', 'increase in terrorism', 'shortage of physicians', 'violence on the street' and 'questions about cancer and the aids treatments' etc. The shattered dreams of the common folk are artistically presented by Gill:

> Beyond
> The bushes of promise
> no castle of vision
> nothing shines from the hills.
> The future seems crumbling
> in a fog of sands. (Gill, *Shrine*, 90)

At the very outset of this research paper, I had tried to exhibit the indelible impression of partition horrors on Stephen gill's psyche. On account of the orgy of violence prevalent in the subcontinent, Gill began to flutter his wings to escape the prison of suffocation. He was in search of an El Dorado of peace. At that time Ethiopia appeared 'an oasis of no fear' to Gill. About his Ethiopian experiences, Gill has written thus in the Preface to *Songs Before Shrine*:

> I received a good income and the climate of Ethiopia was hospitable. I was able to save enough for my further studies and other expenses even after sending money regularly to my mother before she died. (xiii-xiv)

But Gill considered that "Ethiopia was not a country for the writers" So, he came to Canada for doctoral study in English Literature. Even in Canada, he took some time to acclimatize himself to new atmosphere. In a nostalgic mood, he recounts his experiences:

> Even in Canada, nights kept bringing fear with them and sleep kept bringing dreams of soldiers, bulls and the house where I spent my boyhood in New Delhi. I kept dreaming that I was not able to walk forward....Whenever I was in a reflective mood, I condemned myself for deserting my mother when she needed me most.... I kept dreaming of the house where we lived in New Delhi after coming from Pakistan....I continued drinking heavily and also seriously learning the better use of the English language, particularly Canadian English....It took time for me to cross all these stages to become a meaningful writer in a competitive field and country. (Gill, *Songs Before Shrine*, xiv)

So, in the beginning of his career at Canada, he must have faced certain tormenting challenges due to his Asian background. R.K.Singh has raised this issue about Gill in his essay 'Cross-Cultural Communication', where he says:

> As an immigrant writer he, however, tells of the difficulties in making his voice heard. Like many others, Gill suffers in a marginalised existence.... (117)

His novel *Immigrant* depicts the tangling problems which a newcomer to Canada encounters. In a way, the novel is presenting before the readers the psychological strife which Gill faced while settling in Canada. R.K.Singh has aptly pointed out in this connection:

> As he portrays a new Canadian's plight—language barriers, ethnic prejudices, cultural discrepancies and a longing for the motherland—he seems to offer a factual record of his own experiences in Canada. (117)

In an interview given to Jaydeep Sarangi, Gill had himself confessed:

> Every piece of my writing is my child and every child inherits some traits of his or her father. Like any writer, I need material for the construction of my house. The closest place to collect that material is from the field of my own life....It is true that Reghu Nath goes to a University as his Creator goes, and he is from India as his creator is. It is true that *Immigrant* has my blood — it expresses my philosophy on several aspects. (92-93)

To be very precise, through the character of Reghu Nath in the novel, Gill has elaborated the emotional theme of racial prejudice. Here, it will be proper to remark that there are a number of novelists who have portrayed these themes of racial antagonism, East West encounter and alienation in a foreign country. E.M.Forster's *A Passage To India*, Paul Scott's *The Jewel in the Crown* and Raja Rao's *The Serpent and the Rope* are some other important novels, which also talk about this racial prejudice.

In *Immigrant*, the novelist has exhibited the strained relationship between East and West by explicating "the hopes and the fears and the struggle of a newcomer from Indian setting in Canada." The novel also portrays "an insight into the views immigrants hold of white people and vice versa."

The protagonist of the novel Reghu Nath encountered this reality of the racial discord when the receptionists, in the beginning of the second chapter "made no attempt to carry on a conversation... whereas he was anxious to discuss many things with them." (9)

He came to Canada having a rosy picture of the West. The hopes and aspirations of an Indian, who is about to settle in Canada, are realistically portrayed through the character of Reghu Nath:

> He had heard that people in States and Canada were honest and very hard working, as compared to easterners. They abandoned their cars, or sold them to the poor of Asian and African countries at nominal price. He was certain that if he were nice to his Professors one of them would reward him with his car.... Still tossing in bed, he visualised the University, where he would be studying ... He saw Professors and students of both sexes outside classes at social functions, mixing freely and casually. It would be an ideal place, entirely different from those of India where segregation of the sexes was a norm. (10)

Reghu had never been able to express his feelings of love to girls in India due to his shyness. In his fantasy, Reghu visualised that many girls in the West were ready to welcome him "with open arms." (11)

However, the dreams of Reghu are dashed as he finds numberless problems in acclimatising himself to an alien culture. For example, he was asked to telephone the head of the department for an appointment before leaving the University. As he was not aware of the telephone manners, he hesitatingly dialled the number and the call was answered by a lady Professor in 'unintelligible English.' He thought "his student life would be tragic if everyone spoke as she did" (12).The future looked disastrous to him because of this language barrier, created by his ignorance of "the accent or colloquial expression of English speaking countries."

Then entering the registration hall, Reghu Nath felt uncomfortable because he found that everyone except himself was in an informal dress. The novelist paints the predicament of Reghu thus:

> He had come in his business suit, as was the custom of his own country's intelligentsia, who appeared in public well-groomed. He seemed to be the centre of attraction because of his clothes, obviously not tailored in a North American style, and also because he was wearing them in stuffy suffocating weather. (13-14)

In D. Parmeswari's view, "Reghu... experiences a cultural shock, the one that he could least digest." (137) The traumatic experiences of Reghu Nath in Canada are somewhat similar to disturbed emotions of V.S.Naipaul in *The Enigma of Arrival*, a hauntingly brilliant novel about the theme of exile. In the aforesaid novel of Naipaul, the nervousness of the speaker is evident in the following expression:

> After all my time in England, I still had that nervousness in a new place, that rawness of response, still felt myself to be in the other man's country, felt my strangeness, my solitude. And every excursion into a new part of the country—what for others might have been an adventure— was for me like a tearing at an old scab.(13)

Here, it is pertinent to say that the writers of Indian diaspora represent in their writings the psychological problems of dislocation and displacement faced by the immigrants in alien lands. According to Abdul Shamim A.Khan, "The Diasporas also face cultural dilemmas, when their cultural practices are mocked at and there is a threat to their cultural identity." (64) Ranu Uniyal has also analysed the theme of diaspora in the following manner:

> Writers from the Indian Diaspora reflect the yearning and the anxiety of many men and women who continue to feel marginalised and disadvantaged in the developed societies. Subject to racial bias, treated as objects of ridicule because of their dress code, food habits, colour, language and the spoken English, writers tend to expose injustice and inequity through their works.(48)

Stephen Gill's Reghu Nath also finds himself marginalised and disadvantaged in the new social order. The hydra-headed monster of diaspora leaves Reghu's soul wounded. The forlorn lands are just presenting before him the image of 'leaden-eyed despairs'. In a way, he has fallen 'upon the thorns of life'; and 'a heavy weight of hours has chained and bowed' his spirits. Gill presents the tormenting experiences of Reghu Nath thus:

> Within a week, Reghu found himself surrounded with many different problems. Financially, his position was not sound; educationally he did not know where he was headed; psychologically he was not adjusted to his new environment. At the University, he found himself in a mess.... (15)

Similarly, when he held the hand of a compatriot, he quickly found out that it was a sign of perversion in the West. Reghu Nath's awkward position is artistically described by Gill in the following expression:

> After this incident, Reghu began to observe others. He never saw a man holding hands with other men. He also observed men

> seldom shook hands, a very common practice in his country. This affected his own habit of shaking hand warmly and frequently. (20)

Besides, Reghu had come to the West harbouring romantic illusions about the place. He had seen an American movie. The dashing hero of that movie had left an indelible imprint on his psyche. In that movie, the hero told a girl in the first encounter, "I love you." The words of the hero produced the magical effect on the girl; the hero used the same words on several other girls and every time he had the success in winning the hearts of the girls. Gill describes Reghu's imaginary romantic illusions thus:

> He thought it was the way of real life in the west, particularly in America. Reghu had had some love experiences in India, but he was never able to express his feelings to girls. Perhaps it was his shyness or his male ego which stood in his way....In any case, he was now in the West where he was free to practise what he had heard and read. (10-11)

To be very precise, Reghu Nath had the fantasy of many Western girls, welcoming him with open arms. But, these romantic and illusory ideas are dashed to the earth, the moment he reaches the West. The young women puzzled him because they exhibited interest on the first date, but delayed subsequent ones. They were not ready for intimacy too early. Their only interest in becoming friendly with the men was to enjoy life by dinning out and riding in cabs. They never shared the expenses and disliked to be touched on the first date. In a way, the girls were not there with open arms. The approach of these girls is presented realistically in the novel thus:

> Surprisingly, nearly all the girls showed a few characteristics. For instance, they expected to be treated as special, almost as China dolls, and disliked being touched on the first date....If he made any move towards intimacy, it was always the same story, "I do not know you yet" or "We have to understand each other before going further." (22)

Thus, the novel presents the shattering of Reghu's romantic and imaginative illusions about the much hyped west. The Western culture, civilisation and ethos are considered rational, empirical and scientific by the Indians and Reghu Nath is no exception. Talking about Gramscian concept of hegemony, Rajnath too points out in his article "Edward Said and Post Colonial Theory":

> Indians were so brain washed by educational, cultural and religious activities of the West that they began to reckon themselves as inferior and as such developed a propensity for everything Western....(78)

Reghu Nath too had the visions of a glorious West. But his dreams are evaporated, when he reaches Canada. He finds that racial antagonism cannot be easily eliminated from the minds of both the Westerners and Asians. W.F.Westcott has written thus about the conflict of the novel:

> Gill's novel traces Nath's trials and tribulations as he suffers cultural shock, demanding professors, difficult women, Canadian bureaucracy and haunting memories of his native India. Many times, Gill draws on his personal knowledge of Asian life to illustrate Nath's difficulty adapting to a totally foreign racial clime. (116)

Thus, by the above discussion, it is apparent that Gill's work portrays the human misery and anxiety prevalent in the world. Initially Gill found that religious fundamentalism was the root cause of suffering for the people of India and Pakistan. In the Preface to *Songs Before Shrine*, Gill writes about this fire of religious fanaticism:

> Religious mania produces a fire that would continue burning innocent people....This happened when India was divided. That fire forced me to leave India. (xix)

Leaving the subcontinent, he came to Europe. This change of atmosphere could not erase the deep-rooted melancholy from his heart. Here, he found the psychological problems of racial antagonism and biased approach of the natives towards the immigrants. The novel *Immigrant* clearly brings out the problems of Indian diaspora. In Europe too, 'the turbid ebb and flow of human misery' perturbed him.

Now, the question is—Is there a silver lining in the dark clouds of Gill's anxiety over the world issues? Does he provide any remedy for the ills of the society? If we go through his works closely, his prescription for the contemporary society is apparently indicated. In his novel *Immigrant*, he asks for the integration and assimilation of immigrant culture with the ethos and civilisation of the majority community in the West. D. Parmeswari has brilliantly analysed Gill's remedy for the racial antagonism:

> The remedial strategy, which Stephen Gill recommends to a fellow immigrant is integration with the white community, an ideology advocated by another marginalised poet Countee Cullen.... (140)

R.K. Singh has also suggested the presence of the same remedy in *Immigrant*:

> The novel voices the need for openness, for dialogue, for expression of differences and cultural pluralism to minimise misunderstandings, conflicts, exclusiveness and manipulations. (118)

Thus, it is Gill's fervent belief that by promoting the openness of heart, ideals of hybridity and multiculturalism may be developed. The stress on hybrid multicultural and plural world culture may eliminate the vultures of hatred, destruction and confusion. In his emphasis on the mingling of the cultures, Gill comes close to the Britain-based Guyanese writer David Dabydeen. In the view of Dabydeen, London of 1990s "is culturally diverse, but there is little cross-fertilisation of cultures taking place" (qtd. in Rai 16)" Dabydeen adds:

> Very little happens by way of cultural exchange, people cross back to their cells having had a brief encounter with cultural diversity" (qtd. in Rai 16)

Dabydeen has used the image of beehive, while discussing the issue of cultural diversity. In this connection, G.Rai writes:

> Dabydeen, while talking about the cultural diversity of a city like London, uses the image of a 'beehive'. A number of different cultural groups are present in one place with little communication between them taking place. Each is confined to its own cell. Britons do not spend long enough in the West Indian cells nor do they invite West Indians to their cells either. (15-16)

Like Dabydeen, Gill also believes that cultural exchange among the people of various ethnicities and nationalities may eradicate 'the fabric of a crippling chaos.' In a way, through this process, 'the rage of serpent' and 'the lava of hostility' will give way to 'lily of peace.' This stress on the mingling of the cultures is hinted in the following haiku from *Flashes*:

> Nations that extend love
> beyond their boundaries
> bloom boundlessly. (31)

If this process of hybridity is able to survive in the world, the doves of peace will hover over the world. This dove can be visible only when the ethnocentric and jingoistic prejudices are aborted by the people. In the poem, "My Dove", Gill rightly says:

> Underneath her flight
> there are only humans
> no nations. (Gill, *Shrine,* 160)

Dove is a recurrent and all pervading image in Gill's poetry. In the just-mentioned poem, the poet declares:

> She radiates
> hues of undepictable truth
> that sanctify
> the temple of her surroundings.
> The leaf that she carries
> is from the evergreen tree
> of never ending hope.
> The song of her silence
> greets the emergence
> for a cheerful tomorrow. (Gill, *Shrine*, 160)

In another poem "To a Dove", Gill has emotionally painted the dove thus:

> Floating with the free winds
> which leave traces of love
> on our lips and cheeks,
> you accompany the angels
> with your milk-like feathers. (Gill, *Shrine*, 143)

Gill's dove wants to fly above 'the mud of politics.' Its desire is that 'the dance of the hounds' should be stopped. Thus, the dove represents a cheerful tomorrow, which will dawn when there are no human boundaries in the world.

Thus, through the above discussion, it is obvious that Gill's heart is ever crying, as "in the selfish sea of politics/ harmony tosses on wild waves/ endangering boat of justice" (Gill, *Flashes*, 31).He is fed up with religious fury and racial antagonism haunting the nations. He prescribes the remedy of multiculturalism; he asks for the shattering of jingoistic and ethnocentric boundaries to create a new world order, marked by the serene flights of the dove. Due tc this treatment of emotional theme of human predicament in the debased world, Gill has been highly admired by the scholars. For example, Lino Leitao praises him thus: "The message in the poetry of Stephen Gill is harmony" (287). To promote world peace, Gill has advocated world federalism. Hamadan Darwesh has summarised Gill's views about world federalism in the following manner:

> ...the fountain of inspiration for Stephen Gill is world federalism. He believes in forming a democratic one world government to eliminate wars and waste. World federalism has fertilised the thinking of Stephen Gill strongly. (241)

Finally, it may be forcefully asserted that Gill's emotional cries, arising out of religious fanaticism and racial prejudices, are sufficient to give him a permanent place in the history of Indo-Canadian literature. His name will always be written in golden letters in any history of Indian diaspora writers.

Works Cited

Agarwal, N.K. "Stephen Gill on His Writing and Diaspora", *Asian Tribune*. August 13, 2007. December 6, 2007. <http://www.asiantribune.com/index.php?q=node/6943>.

Anand, Mulk Raj. "The Aesthetic Hypothesis", *Indian Aesthetics: An Introduction*. Ed. V.S.Seturaman. Chennai: Macmillan, 1992. 384-397.

Choudhary, Satya Dev. *Glimpses of Indian Poetics*. New Delhi: Sahitya Akademi, 2002.

Darwesh, Hamadan. "A Study of Faiz Ahmed Faiz and Stephen Gill", *Glimpses*. Ed. Hamadan Darwesh. Ontario: Vesta, 2005. 238- 247.

Eliot, T.S. "Yeats", 1940. *Selected Prose*. Ed. John Hayward. Harmondsworth: Penguin, 1953. 186-193.

Gill, Stephen. *Immigrant*. Ontario:Vesta,1982.

__________. *Shrine*. Arizona: World University Press, 1999.

__________. *Flashes*. New Delhi: Imprint, 2007.

__________. *Songs Before Shrine*. Delhi: Authorspress, 2007.

Iyengar, K.R.S. *Indian Writing in English.* 5th ed. New Delhi: Sterling, 1985.

Khan, Abdul S.A. "The Indian Diaspora in Canada: A Note on Rohinton Mistry", *Spiel Journal of English Studies* 1.2 (2005): 63-68.

Lahiri, Tapiti. "Amrinder's *Lajo* and Taslima Nasrin's *Lajja* as Political Novels", *Points of View* 2.1 (1995): 94-101.

Leitao, Lino. "The Concept of Harmony in the Ojibways of Canada And the Poetry of Stephen Gill", *Glimpses.* Ed. Hamadan Darwesh. Ontario: Vesta, 2005. 276-289.

Mohan, G.B. *The Response To Poetry: A Study in Comparative Aesthetics.* New Delhi: People's Publishing House, 1968.

Naipaul, V.S. *The Enigma of Arrival.* Harmondsworth: Penguin, 1987.

Narayan, Shyamala A. and John Mee. "Novelists of the 1950s and 1960s", *An Illustrated History of Indian Literature in English.* Ed. Arvind Krishna Mehrotra. Delhi: Permanent Black, 2003. 219- 231.

Parmeswari, D. "The Cultural Baggage: A Reading of Stephen Gill's Immigrant", *Glimpses.* Ed.Hamadan Darwesh.Ontario: Vesta, 2005. 135-141.

Rai, G. "Post Colonialism: Its Meaning and Significance", *Spiel Journal of English Studies* 1.2 (2005): 1-22.

Rajnath. "Edward Said And Postcolonial Theory", *Journal of Literary Criticism* 9.1 (2000): 73-87.

Sarangi, Jaydeep. "Interview with Stephen Gill", 2004. *Glimpses.* 90-103.

Shahane, V.A. "Khushwant Singh: An Artist in Realism", *Critical Essays on Indian Writing in English.* Eds. M. K. Naik, S. K. Desai and G.S. Amur. Silver Jubilee Students Edition. Madras: Macmillan, 1977. 344-355.

Singh, R.K. "Cross-Cultural Communication", 1998. *Glimpses.* 117-122.

Uniyal, Ranu. "Associating Difference With Diversity: Writers from the Indian Diaspora", *Spiel Journal of English Studies* 1.2 (2005): 45- 54.

Walsh, William. *Indian Literature in English.* London: Longman, 1990.

Westcott, W.F. "Immigrant", *Glimpses.* 116.

Yeats, W.B. *Collected Poems.* Rupa Paperback Edition. Calcutta: Rupa. 1993.

13

Stephen Gill on His Writing and Diaspora: An Interview

—Nilanshu Kumar Agarwal

> Every time there was a stir caused by the wind, a car on the street, the bark of a dog, or the mew of a cat, we froze inside our house. Every time there was anything unusual, unseen tragedy was expected. The nights were nightmares and the days did not bring any hope. Often the mornings dawned with more lamentable events. It was not easy to sleep when night after night the ghosts of fear looked straight into our eyes.

The aforesaid pathetic statement about the condition of post-partition India in the year 1947 by the poet laureate of Ansted University, Stephen Gill, shows his deep concern for the humanity. This man of high poetic sensibility has authored more than twenty books, including novels, literary criticism and collections of poems. His poetry and prose have appeared in more than five hundred publications mostly in Canada, U.S.A. and India.

Stephen Gill, a member of several prestigious organisations like The PEN, the Writer's Union of Canada, Amnesty International and Associated Church Press, was born in Sialkot, Pakistan, and grewup in India. After teaching in Ethiopia for three years, he migrated to England before settling in Canada. Due to his relationship with so many countries, his poetry represents the contemporary world which is variously called as 'a melting pot' or 'a salad bowl'. His poetry presents a true picture of this mingling of the cultures. Moreover, his verse is a sort of bridge between India and Pakistan.

An advisor to several publications, Gill has edited several publications including the Canadian section of the *World Federation Newspaper*, *Writer's Lifeline* and *South Christian Diary*. This man of versatile genius talks to Dr.Nilanshu Kumar Agarwal about Indian Diaspora in Canada, problems of English studies in India, haiku poetry, his own literary sensibility and several other relevant contemporary issues in a detailed and pedantic interview. On account of his long association with several literary and academic organisations, Gill has presented his erudite views about English studies in India. Through this conversation, he has very objectively analysed the condition of English studies in India and has also given his suggestions for the improvement of English studies in India along with a number of other issues related to contemporary world, literature and society.

NKA: Wordsworth defined poetry as spontaneous overflow of powerful feelings. Whereas T.S.Eliot went against the emotions and exclaimed: "Poetry is not a turning loose of emotions, but an escape from emotions". What is the best way? Should a poet be subjective or objective? Or, should there be a perfect balance between the two? Which path do you prefer in your poetry? Please communicate.

SG: Poetry is a spiritual and psychic experience. To give shape to this experience, poets need special knowledge in order to use images, tone, economy of words and other techniques. To weave a rainbow of beauty poets select and adjust words in different combinations.

Poetry is neither "emotions recollected in tranquillity," nor is it "turning loose of emotions." Poetry is experience that can happen any time with or without reason. One element that is common in both definitions, and in most others, is the presence of emotions. I will call these emotions airy beings. With their tools poets catch the airy beings in the net of their words. It is like catching fish in a sea. Painters catch them in the net of their colours with the hands of their brushes. Dancers catch them in the net of the movements with their hands, eyes, brows and other body parts. These are different techniques that do the same work.

Poets train themselves to catch airy beings. I call these airy beings the robins of my art in my preface to *The Flame*. There I say that these robins are not meant to be caged. They are the birds of freedom. They enjoy their freedom when poets send them to publications or present them in a book for the enjoyment of the reader.

In my poem "Oars", I call them "naked creatures of waves." A poet "clothes them with images / stitched with words" (*Songs Before Shrine,* 36*)*. Poets are wordsmiths, who have knowledge and education about the tools that are used to clothe these airy beings in a graceful way. This is an art. A person may be born with a propensity to be a poet, but that is not enough. Propensity or talent is like a raw diamond that has to be chiselled and polished into a beautiful form. In order to acquire the knowledge of chiselling and polishing a poet needs work that I call perspiration. To me poetry is seventy-five per cent perspiration and twenty-five per cent inspiration or talent. Perspiration needs struggle to know how to use the tools of a poet effectively.

NKA: What are the major themes of your poetry?

SG: The major theme of my poetry is peace. Peace is the absence of war or fear of war and bloodshed. My poems about peace are about the definition of peace, in favour of harmony, against war and bloodshed, and to condemn terrorism. I believe that peace is the legitimate child of peaceful means. I deal with subjects such as war, bloodshed, harmony, human rights, and democracy. Some poems about peace from my collection *Shrine* include "Peace of Mind", "To a Dove", "Flight of a Dove", "My House of Peace", and "My Dove". From *Songs Before Shrine,* I would like to include "Peace" , "Dove of Peace," "My Name is Peace", "Seeking the Dove of Peace", "Harmony and Peace", "Evening of Harmony", "Rays of Harmony", "When", "Harmony", "Muse of Peace", "Where are They", "Prince of Peace", and "Domain of Peace". These poems are directly related to my major theme. The poems that condemn terrorism include "Religious Fanaticism" and "Terrorists" from *Shrine*. My long poem, The *Flame*, that is of 152 pages and divided into sixty two cantos, is about terrorism and peace. In addition to these poems, there are references to terrorism in other poems.

I have written and published poems also in Urdu and Punjabi against terrorism. I have a number of poems on other social concerns, including AIDS, children and discriminations. Notable poems to condemn war include "Talking of Peace", "War Fever", "Arms Trader", "Hounds of War", "My Beliefs", and "Last Dance" from *Shrine.* "If There Be a Third World War", "A Question", "To WarMongers", "War is Fraud", "About War" are a few notable poems from *Songs Before Shrine*.

There is a complete section to condemn war in *Flashes,* a collection of my haiku. In addition, I have edited two anthologies of poems, titled *Anti-War Poems*, volume one and volume two. Volume one was released in 1984. It has one hundred and twenty contributors from seven nations. Volume Two was released in 1986. It has over one hundred poets from seventeen nations. In both the anthologies, poets condemn war.

We are breathing in an exceedingly perilous atmosphere that is deteriorating at an alarming speed. One single factor that is responsible for this impending peril is nuclear warfare, hanging over our heads like the Sword of Damocles to destroy us all. Scientists so far have not been able to discover any other civilisation anywhere else in the universe. If by any chance the nuclear giant is out, even this single civilisation of ours will be wiped out, leaving the sun, the moon and the stars to appear and disappear without anyone being to enjoy their sight. It has taken centuries to build our civilisation and it will take minutes to annihilate the same. Obviously, it would be an inexpressible tragedy.

The poems of anti-war anthologies are related directly to war and peace. In addition to these poems, there are several more that have references to war and bloodshed. I have also written several poems condemning war and bloodshed in Urdu and Punjabi languages.

I have also tackled the problem of war and peace in my prose. There are several articles to condemn war and bloodshed. I have given talks and interviews on radio and television. Some of these interviews have been collected in a DVD, titled *Interviews of Stephen Gill*.

Writers and poets are involved with every aspect of life, including news media, and creative arts. The heart is the seat for peace. If the heart is at peace, the world around can also be impacted with the radiance of peace emitted by eyes, tongue and actions. .

Poets are involved with many aspects of life, like writing songs and speeches for politicians and business executives. Lorca and Byron gave their lives for the cause of liberation. Among the written documents, the *Vedas*, the *Bible*, and the *Koran* have a great impact on the minds of people. Lately, Pentagon papers concerning the Vietnam War have changed the thinking of several Americans, and a book titled *Uncle Tom's Cabin* by Harriet Beecher Stowe was partly responsible for the liberation of the slaves in the USA. I hope that my writings about peace will cause change in the thinking of my readers.

There are different aspects of peace, including terrorism, human rights, bloodshed, and poverty. I deal with them in an art form. This art form is as important to me as is the theme. To write a good poem on peace, I concentrate deeply to select the right words and tone, and to weed out excessive fat.

Writing is also therapeutic to me. In order to give light, a candle burns itself. That is what a poet does. I write to disseminate my message in an art form. This is a process of burning oneself or going through the pains of a pregnant mother.

A poem should not be predictable, and it should not be constructed on the trodden path. In other words, the emotions should be caught in the meshes of a style that is devoid of emotional clichés and redundancies. The word clichés refers to expressions that have been used excessively and become stale. In other words, a cliché is an idea, a metaphor or an expression that has lost its freshness because it has been used frequently. Such expressions are often heard and read and a poet is likely to lose admirers.

I try to use fresh language and images; I am cautious to use allusions that are hackneyed. Trite expressions are often used in Indian English Literature, such as Ram Rajya, apple's eyes, at a stone's throw, a faithful friend, Mother Nature, leave no stone unturned, wear and tear, axe to grind, nip in the bud and many more. These are worn-out phrases. Sometimes, original expressions may be obscure to the reader and may prove enigmatic. It is sometimes baffling for me to choose between a private image that is original and trite expressions that are over-familiar. However, there are times when it becomes important to use a cliché for brevity or clarity. Such incidents may be rare. It is not easy to put emotions into words and images that are imaginative and inventive. All these requirements need revisions.

I also pay a special attention to tone. Tone is the voice of a speaker that tells if the speaker is angry, preachy, scornful, and so on. Just a simple sentence "I need you," may have different meanings to different listeners, depending on the tone of the voice and if the speaker has a smile or any other expression on his voice. The tone can be understood but difficult to interpret. It can be soft, loud, whispering and even scornful.

Tone is the prevailing spirit, or the moral attitude, of the poet towards his reader. A poet conveys the tone in his poems through words and expressions. It is difficult to express it in a poem. In order to convey the right tone, a poet needs revision to select the right expressions.

Poems that are preachy are not admired much. One can be preachy without being obvious. If I have to preach something, I use prose. Poetry is an aesthetic art and I want to keep it that way. I use peace as a subject matter and toil to handle it as a piece of art. Art is beauty. When I read a poem, I look for aesthetic qualities, not for information and knowledge. For knowledge or information, I will read books in prose. This is what readers expect. Therefore I avoid being preachy in my poetry. I believe that to achieve peace, the best means are the peaceful means. If I have to preach, I will use the media of prose, where I can use logic and reasoning to get my message across.

Art is a way of expression that can assume the shape of visual, performing or literary art. All these arts express culture that can be personal or collective. Expression is life-breath — the palpitation of a nation or an individual. Poetry is an art of expression and expression differs as does the appearance of individuals.

When a person perceives an object—beautiful or ugly—it produces a reaction or feelings. Those feelings, reactions or sentiments are formless. A poet expresses those formless objects in a sensible form. One can use a cliché that is easy and needs no effort, but there is no inventiveness in its use. One can find new ways and modes to express the object. That needs real effort. That is called individual approach—a distinctive element—fresh memorable piece of art. Such a treatment needs intellectual exercise. A poet has to manage an unmanageable horse of emotions that needs skills, guidance and control to be able to achieve smooth efficient operation of a poem. In order to achieve this object, a poet needs time to work in different ways to bring those feelings out. In other words, it needs revisions. Let me also emphasize that poetry is as demanding as any art is. It demands devotion, skill and professionalism.

NKA: You have authored a haiku collection entitled *Flashes*. What are your views about this type of poetry?

SG: I became interested in haiku in 1988, when I began to study poets from the point of their form and style. Some of them had been haiku writers. Haiku enamoured me as I went deeper in its study, savouring its delightful simple presence though its simplicity is deceptive.

By its very nature a haiku is an unfinished poem, written in telegraphic language. A traditional haiku is of three lines, and has definite syllables of five, seven and five respectively. It also suggests a season. All that I can say is that haiku is mostly the bones of an experience or revelation.

Haiku was born in Japan and is still admired there. Several new trends, particularly in English haiku, have been introduced over the years. Haiku also strengthened the symbolist movement in France and Imagists in English literature between 1912 and 1918. Notable imagists were F.S. Flint, Pound, Amy Lowell and John Gould Fletcher. They attacked the emotional and excessive use of the metric verse of the time.

Because of its brevity, a haiku can be jotted down in short intervals. Moreover, haiku poets do not have to be tied to set rules. They can write on highly unusual as well as on ordinary aspects of life. A haiku does not have to be about special moments. What can be more joyful than to be able to find beauty in everything around without waiting for something rare to happen. This element turns haiku into daily bread, not a feast to be enjoyed on specific occasions. For the writers of haiku, the well of imagination never goes dry. They do not have to go to a library in search of material, nor do they have to shut themselves in their rooms to explore the chambers of their minds. This is because the material is right in front of them, even when they look into the mirror. To illustrate how easy it is to catch these ideas from daily life, I will quote my two haiku verses:

> Dishes clutter the table
> light smiles from above
> house is silent.

The above three lines sketch an ordinary scene from ordinary life. This scene from a kitchen suggests a family get-together, when all the guests have gone, leaving the dishes on the table to be picked up for washing. It is late evening, suggested by a light, and the silence indicates that the hosts have gone to bed because they may be tired. They may do the dishes the next day. Here is another haiku of mine:

> Without you
> I am a leafless tree
> love is the sap. (Stephen Gill)

For haiku writers material is everywhere. They find material even in the most mundane situations. To them style is a dress as it is for humans. A poet may say that he or she has no problem finding material; it is the choice of words or diction they have to struggle with. For haiku poets such distinctions do not exist. They use ordinary language to present their ordinary life. Many haiku poems appear primarily prosaic, like Basho's diaries.

Several English haiku writers have used rhyme successfully, but its use is not essential. Over the years, a vast body of haiku has been produced, and still is being produced, in which rhyme has been used rarely. This choice makes the job of haiku poets easier.

Haiku has been free enough to adjust itself to the needs of poets of every succeeding age under different circumstances. For instance, in Japan, Yosa Buson (1716-1783) introduced a more personal style. Kobayashi Issa (1763-1827) introduced a popular note, using haiku to portray human misery and absurdity and to evoke compassion for man's weaknesses. In modern times, haiku has received fresh waters from Masaoka Shiki and Takayama Kyoshi. In the West, haiku has influenced poets in different ways. As the *Encyclopaedia of Poetry and Poetics* states, Western poets interested in it knew no Japanese, and therefore produced results which often had little to do with haiku.

Haiku entices the poets who dislike original limitations, particularly concerning the use of syllabic versification, reference to season and terse language. Temperamentally, I cannot develop a love for something that is chained. I like to be free like nature itself. That may be why the wind and dove in various shapes appear in my poetry. Moreover, I do not perceive much creativity in work in which a poet has to struggle to conform to the established norms. Haiku offers freedom to freedom-loving poets. For them, there are vast possibilities for adopting new techniques.

I am not among those poets who finish off several pieces in a single sitting. Rather I am a slow but steady producer. My first draft is a diamond in a rough shape. I polish and chisel, a practice that is against the teachings of Basho.

Bashu Matsuo, the first great master of haiku, was born in Japan in 1644 and died in 1694. He was influenced by a fourth-century B.C. philosopher, Tchouang-tsen, who believed that the real value lies in useless things, and the right way of life is to accept and follow the laws of nature.

Distractions do not pose serious problems for haiku poets, though all writers hate them no matter how deeply they are in love with writing. Interruptions are unable to irritate haiku poets because they only need a few minutes to jot down three lines, anywhere, any time. The novelists and poets of other genres may envy haiku writers for this very reason. Even if writers inform the other members of their families not to interrupt them at certain hours, the family may not know what this means because distraction or interruption has different connotations for different people. When a writer goes to the washroom or to the kitchen for a glass of water, the spouse and children may think that the writer is now open for conversation. This sort of problem does not bother a haiku writer.

One way for a poet to make the best possible use of any available time is to get hold of a pocket-sized tape-recorder. Inspiration comes as a flash, a revelation. A poet should put it into words immediately. Otherwise, it will fade or evaporate sooner than water does in a tropical country. Such flashes happen seldom. They seem to be a result of the poet's unconscious acts. Priceless gems, which are the works of this unconscious mind, may be lost by procrastination. I have lost many gems. In my long drives, I keep a tape-recorder within reach to pick up for recording. It is small enough to fit in any coat pocket, and is easy to operate, without even looking at it. Anything recorded can be revised and polished later. What can be more fun than catching daily scenes and random thoughts in three lines! It is a different matter if a poet happens to be too lazy to pick up a notebook and a pen. If this seems to be a problem, I would advise such a poet to keep a mini tape-recorder all the time in his or her pocket. If they cannot even do this, then, I would ask them to look within, to know if they are eligible suitors for the muse. Maybe, they will do better as plumbers, or at the grocery store, than as priests in the temple of haiku.

Everyone likes short cuts, no matter where he or she goes. So do writers, to save time. Fortunately, haiku poets do not need these short cuts. Haiku itself is a short cut to writing full poems of several lines. Haiku is one of the oldest forms of poetry and therefore it has had a long time to mature, going through several stages of experimentation not only in Japan, where it was born, but also in the West. Haiku has become flexible enough for new temperaments, modes of thought and expressions. A poet can adapt it to suit his or her personality and philosophy. Haiku has become a hat which has lost its original shape because it has been worn on heads of different sizes. Yet it looks new and attractive. With a few adjustments, this hat can be worn by any poet.

To study my views about haiku further and from another angle, I would suggest reading my introduction to *Flashes,* a collection of my haiku. This introduction is also on my website: www.stephengill.ca.

NKA: A number of Indian students, pursuing even post-graduation in English fail to comprehend English, language properly. This proliferation of ignorance about English language is creating a sort of digital divide, as most of the researches in the field of Information Technology are done in English language. The gulf between the computer literates and computer illiterates is widening because of this ignorance about the intricacies of language. So, should not we fill this gap by teaching the students the minutest details of English language in place of lecturing on a number of irrelevant colonial texts of England? Please make your illuminating comments.

SG: The answer to this relevant question is easy, but the czars in India will not like to solve it. They are likely to agree with it. The answer would slip their power into the hands of millions of others who aspire to touch the pinnacle of progress. These czars have studied in English-speaking schools and have the means to send their children to these schools. These schools provide an environment to children in which they can develop self-confidence in early years. They fare much better in universities because of their early education and also compete easily at the examinations for top positions. Because these czars do not want those positions to be made available to everyone, they will not do anything to improve the situation. They may come up with theories. For example, they may say that the economically backward classes have sinned in their previous lives and therefore are being punished.

I have discussed the question of English in my introduction to *The Flame*. I am from the government-run schools where English is touched at the minimum level. Such schools are useless for India if she wants to compete in the global village of today.

Let me bring out a recent incident. I had a problem with my computer here in Canada. When I phoned Microsoft, I was connected with an assistant in Bangalore, India. When he was not able to solve the problem, he gave me Wednesday to discuss the problem further. I told the assistant that the coming Wednesday was a bad day for me.

He could not understand why that day was bad for me. He thought that I was superstitious. It is a North American expression that meant I was busy that Wednesday. But he took it in a different sense. I have discussed such problems in my novel *Immigrant.* I am sure researchers would find this novel useful.

I have the following suggestions:

1. The government-run schools should have one or two periods exclusively devoted to the speaking of the English language. This should be right from the early years. Students should be encouraged to listen to speeches by English-speaking foreigners, and teachers should ask students questions based on those speeches. It should be all oral. Language comes by listening and speaking.

2. At the university level, there should be fifty per cent marks set aside for participation in seminar classes. Students should write term papers and present them to the class for discussion. Based on those discussions, students should be evaluated. To evaluate just on the basis of examinations that are held once a year is not a balanced approach.

3. I would suggest that every university should hire at least one foreign teacher for the subject of English.

4. The concept of hiring a poet or writer from an English-speaking nation every year for at least a few months should be encouraged. These writers are available for the students and professors for consultation for their writing and publishing problems. Colleges and universities in Canada, the USA and UK have such programmes. These programmes not only help students and teachers, but also bring name to the institutions. When a prominent writer or poet is invited for even six months at a time, the students flock to that university or college. At the same time, that writer will have time to do some of his research work or creative writing while at the campus. Such positions are called poets in residence or writers in residence. There is almost nothing like this in Indian universities.

NKA: What are the psychological problems of Indian diaspora in Canada? Like Ruth in Keats's "Ode to a Nightingale", Indian diaspora must be "in tears amid the alien corn", as they harbour the memories of Indian past and are not completely acclimatised to new culture. What are your ideas about this traumatic experience of Indian diaspora in Canada?

SG: The story of Ruth that John Keats mentions is from the *Old Testament* in the *Bible*. Ruth married a man from Judea, more or less Israel now, in her homeland Moab where he moved when his country was attacked by a famine. After the death of her husband, Ruth, still childless, moved to Judea with her mother-in-law Noami. The days of famine were over. The story of Ruth has been recorded in the *Bible* because of her unsurpassed loyalty to her mother-in-law who was Jewish. Ruth told her mother-in-law, "I want to go where you go and live where you live. I want your people to be my people and your God to be my God."

In Judea, while gleaning the barley harvest, Ruth met a man named Boaz, a relative of Noami, who owned that field. He was captivated by the beauty, modesty and piety of Ruth. They fell in love and in course of time got married. She bore a son that Noami took care of. That child was the progenitor of Christ and the great grandfather of King David. This happened about three thousand years ago. In that field Ruth thought of Moab, her homeland. It is notable that it was her devotion to her mother-in law that was the ruling factor in her decision to migrate to Judea.

There was another diaspora before Ruth and that was soon after God created the world. That was the first diaspora in the recorded history of the *Bible*. In the beginning, God created Adam and Eve and gave them a beautiful place to live in, called the Garden of Eden. He allowed them sovereignty over everything, except over a particular tree. They violated the commandment of God and tasted the forbidden fruit of that tree. As a result, they were forced out of that garden to work hard for their living.

Adam and Eve must have repented for violating the law of God. In the second life of hard work, they must have remembered the good old days when life was pleasing amidst trees, flowers and animals without day-to-day worries about food and shelter.

In the story of Ruth, diaspora was due to devotion and loyalty. Ruth must have been caught between her love for her homeland and her love for her mother-in-law. She must have suffered because she was torn between two passions. Ruth as well as Adam and Eve are diasporans.

Diaspora in Hebrew means exile (*Jeremiah*: 24:5), that is "expulsion of a national from his country by the government or voluntary removal of a citizen, usually in order to escape punishment". (*The Columbia Encyclopaedia*). Diaspora has been mentioned in the *Old Testament* also as punishment. In *Deuteronomy* Xxviii; xxx11, dispersion of the Jews among nations is foretold as punishment for their apostasy. In the book of *Deuteronomy* (28:25) it is written: "thou shall be a diaspora in all kingdoms of the earth." The Jews were exiled from Judea in 586 BCE by Babylonians and Jerusalem in 135 CE by the Roman Empire. They travelled with their own luggage. Their dislocation, homelessness and memories of their homeland were part of the diasporic sensibility. Sufferings in a new land under a new rule and geographical conditions and inability to go back were the important features of the diaspora of the Jews.

Jews suffered in the twentieth century when the Nazis came to power in Germany and set up concentration camps for their torture. Around seven million Jews were killed. Even after their homeland was formed, their sufferings did not come to an end. It is estimated that around 90,000 Jews from Arab countries dispersed to different parts of the world, mostly to Europe and North America.

In all these stories exile was under compulsion. In the story of Ruth, it was the compulsion by the devotion that she had for her mother-in law. Later this compulsion became a bond when she married a local man in her adopted land, Judea. This bond became much stronger when a son was born. Due to these powerful bonds she was not free to go back to the land of her birth. Her inability to go back to her land of birth, Moab, was complicated by the distance. For a woman to cover a journey of two or three days alone with luggage about three thousand years ago was beset with unimaginable hazards. She must have become nostalgic now and then because she was among foreigners.

The present use of the word diaspora about Canadian writers who were not born In India Is loaded with confusions. Its overuse or loose use conflicts with words like immigrant, refugee, visitor, racial minorities, ethnic groups and so on. Some writers include nearly every one who was born outside the country and talks about the country of origin. If diaspora is analyzed in the light of its original use that was for the Jews and even the major diasporas of non-Jews, it becomes necessary to include the elements of alienation, loss, forced migration, memories of the past and a dream to return to the land of birth. It may include also the unwilling acceptance of the host country.

Academic studies of diaspora began to be popular in the late twentieth century. Diaspora happened in several nations and ethnic groups throughout the history of humankind. In addition to the Jewish diaspora, other major diasporas are from Africa and Armenia. The Indian diaspora started mainly after the British made her a part of the empire. Indians were moved as forced labour in the nineteenth century to other parts of the empire, including Fiji, Mauritius, Guyana, Trinidad, Surinam, and Malaysia. Canada has a sizeable number of immigrants of Indian origin from African and Caribbean nations. Neither they nor their parents were born in India. In some cases even their grandparents were not born in India. Except for their appearance and in some instances their first or last names, they have nothing to do with India.

Diasporans maintain continuous contact with their homeland and with other dispersed segments of the same group. There is no such thing on an organised basis in Canada. Ethnic writers do not have an organisation of their own to remain in touch with one another.

An important factor has been brought out by *Food and Culture Encyclopaedia* that says, "A key characteristic of diaspora is that a strong sense of connection to a homeland is maintained through cultural practices and ways of life. Among these culinary culture has an important part to play in diasporic identifications."

Any immigrant group from any nation who uses neither Indian dresses nor enjoys any Indian food on a routine basis should not be identified as Indian diaspora. Food habits and language are the key constituents of diaspora. Not only that, the culture of several immigrants who were not born in India is a mixture of identities. They can hardly understand any Indian language and hardly prepare any Indian food at home. It is the culture that bonds a group and culture includes language and food habits. Religion has never been a unifying force in the history of humankind nor the last or the first name of a person.

Some immigrant writers cry over discrimination in Canada, whereas the fact is that there was no discrimination in the country of their birth that forced them to settle abroad. They had no problem as forced exiled people have. Their tears in Canada are of a political nature. They enjoy shedding tears because there are sympathetic ears to listen to them. Sometimes, it helps to receive awards from governments on the basis of sympathy.

Book publishers are in business to make money. They look for sensational material that is available in India at every corner. They also guide their authors how to sensationalise particular stories. The authors of such books are not there as prophets or on any mercy or peace mission. They also want to exploit situations. The result is exaggeration in the novels of such fiction writers to make them interesting. Such descriptions should not be confused with memories of their past in India.

Diaspora and nostalgic memories are inseparable. Ruth in Keats' "Ode to Nightingale" must have thought of her land of birth nostalgically. It was natural for Ruth to be nostalgic about the country where her sister and parents lived and where she passed her childhood and a part of her youth. There was no exoticism or marketing involved. "Exoticism, by definition, is the charm of the unfamiliar" (*Wikipedia)*. How can these immigrant writers think of India when they never lived there, except for their occasional literary trips? There is almost nothing in their writing about India or even about the land of their birth that can be constituted as nostalgic. Their description of India is to exoticise for marketing purpose. To group them under Indian diaspora is going too far. It is better to call them immigrants or ethnic or Afro-Asian or Afro-Indian writers.

Diasporans in history had diaries in which they recorded the hard life in the lands of their birth. They often talked and wrote against the laws and prejudices in the land of their birth. Because those factors were responsible for their exile, they attacked them. Being from the majority or financially and educationally stronger groups in the countries of their birth, these Canadian ethnic groups did not experience discrimination in their homelands. That is why there is nothing worth noting about discrimination in the writings of these Canadian immigrant writers. They hardly know India and therefore cannot write, except about the caste system and things like that in general.

Discrimination is an important part of diaspora, because it is largely the discrimination in the country of birth that forces them to seek refuge abroad. In the country of birth, this discrimination becomes life-threatening or intolerable. In the host country it is not life-threatening and obvious. If they find discrimination in Canada, they can easily go back. Several immigrants hold dual citizenships. They come and go to the countries of their birth, not India.

Second generation children should not be included in the category of diaspora. The new generation cannot be nostalgic about the country they only hear, read or see on the TV screens like any other country and any person. If their children are the outcome of mixed marriages between different ethnic groups, they should not be called diasporans. Such children cannot stay in the country of their parents more than a couple of weeks. Ruth was a diasporan also because of her affectionate memories. But her son who was born and brought up in Judea was not a diasporan. He had nothing to be nostalgic about. He may have had a soft corner for the country of his mother, but nothing more than that.

The immigrants who go abroad in search of green pastures cannot be diasporans, because they are free to go back. Their migration is not a diaspora, because skilled and professional immigrants, including medical doctors, engineers, nurses and investors are under no compulsion to leave their country. Most newcomers in the nations of greener pastures bid farewell to their lands of birth because of their loyalty to the god of gold. Suffering from the mania of petrodollars, they search for an El Dorado of prosperity for themselves and their children in Europe and North America. They keep sending their dollars back home where they buy land or invest in business. Most of them cannot adjust to the life back home. They come and go whenever they want and eventually settle in Canada, enjoying the best of both worlds. Inability to go back and unwilling acceptance of the new country were also important factors that constituted the original diaspora in the history of humankind. The diaspora of the Jews, Armenians and African slaves have set criterion that these ethnic newcomers to Canada do not meet.

Under a close examination of the definition and origin of diaspora, most ethnic writers of Canada are not diasporans, because their knowledge of India is based on the movies and news items from the media. Their knowledge is not better than the knowledge of several whites who for one reason or the other are interested in India. Those who were not born in India, not even their parents, should not be called Indian diasporans, because they are not in touch with India; they keep their contacts with the country of their birth that may be a Caribbean or an African nation.

These economic refugees carry their luggage of colour and habits that are peculiar to the nations where they were born. They buy lands in the land of their origin, visit them periodically, have their children married there and want the best of both worlds. They have nothing to do with India, except their appearance, or their first or last name. Their women do not have any idea of Sarees, and Indian food, except chicken curry and ladoos. In some cases, the whites have more knowledge about India than they have.

Considering the barometer that is used here, most immigrant writers of Canada should not be classified as diasporans and their literary output as diaspora. Moreover, they are not "in tears amid alien corn". Modern India is an awakening giant after a long slumber. Some Afro-Asian or Afro-Indian writers of Canada want to be associated with India that has a long tradition to welcome everyone. Association is one thing and to be diaspora or a diasporan another.

NKA: In this dismal world, haunted by 'blood dimmed tide' of chaotic disorder, what is the significance of literature?

SG: Literature is communication, and communication is the oxygen of life. Even animals and plants communicate in their own way. Human communication is of a highly developed nature.

Communication in healthy literature is through artistic beauty, and beauty is peace. The opposite of beauty is ugliness, and ugliness embodies violence. Literature is by humans, for humans. The relation of humans to literature is the same that is between sound and music. Good healthy literature is a candle that spreads the fragrance of light. There are persons who are allergic to this fragrance. They want to put out this candle. They are sick. Violence is the expression of sick minds, to uproot life, to kill communication.

Healthy literature takes humans to a higher level of communication. Artistic beauty deepens the awareness of life and its fruits of blessedness. The world is filled with fruits, trees and flowers in every shape and colour for humans to celebrate these beauties. It is the human who has poisoned these beauties and made the world a dismal place.

NKA: You have inculcated the culture of various countries. Has this diversity of experience influenced you poetry? I suppose this multiplicity of experience must have made your poetic idiom multi-coloured. What are the effects of this cultural rainbow on you language? Does not your language resemble 'a salad bowl' or 'a melting pot' due to this diversity of experience? Please enlighten.

SG: Persons are shaped in the smithy of their environment. Being a citizen of the global village, I am influenced also from diverse directions. The first influence that has shaped my outlook was my childhood in New Delhi at the time of the division of India, when the blood of the innocent cried for sanity.

I agree there is individuality in my work. It certainly has to do with my childhood, the books I read, and the countries I have visited and lived in. When Westerners read my work, they say there is Eastern wisdom. When people from the East read, they say there is Western influence. My poetry is neither Eastern nor Western—my outlook does not represent a nation or a creed, nor any school or thought. I follow truth as I perceive it because truth sets a person free. I write to share this truth with others.

To express myself for sharing in an artistic form, I struggle to find the means that are beautiful and easy to grasp by most. The audience that I have in mind is the audience of the global village, including intellectuals as well as common man, though it is not easy to find an expression that is for all. Moreover, I try to avoid worn-out expressions. I leave it to my readers to find out if my work is a salad bowl.

However, according to the medical science, salad blossoms a richness of nutrients for calm energy to surge healthy hormones.

NKA: Tell something about your recent work *Songs Before Shrine.*

SG: *Songs Before Shrine* is off the press, and I have said enough about this collection in my author's preface. I would like to add that *The Flame* is my most ambitious work. Next to it is *Shrine. Songs Before Shrine* is third in this order, though every book, like a child to the mother, is important to the author for one reason or the other. This is my personal opinion. Readers and critics may have their own opinions. John Milton liked his epic *Paradise Regained* more than his epic *Paradise Lost.* Today, he is known for *Paradise Lost.*

NKA: Macaulay propagated the study of English literature (Literature of England), as he wanted to colonise the Indian mind. Thinkers like Foucault, Gramsci and Edward Said have focussed on the hegemony of the West in converting the ideologies of the colonies by educating the colonised the cultural values of the coloniser. So, is it not the task of the academia in India and other former colonies of the West to decolonise English studies in their lands? Why should we go on teaching Chaucer, Ben Jonson, Galsworthy, Orwell and D.H.Lawrence etc. to our students? Is it not better to teach them our own classics in English language? Your views, please.

SG: Indian languages have their own classics. I am sure those Indian classics are part of the curriculum of those languages. There is no point in teaching them in India in English translation.

Classical literature of English, like literature in any language, is communication at a higher level. Opportunities should be made available to the students who want to develop their English skills and knowledge by studying its best writers. There is nothing wrong with knowing the literature of the English language, because English is also a language of India now, and is becoming more and more important in day-to-day life. India is a part of the global village and therefore it would not help India to shut her doors to other cultures.

India has produced some good writers in English that include India-born overseas poets and fiction writers. Indian institutes of learning should pay them special attention, considering them as valuable assets.

NKA: Information Technology has entered into every sphere of life. There are concepts like e-governance, e-commerce, e-business and e-learning. What is the role of IT in the furtherance of literary activity? Is the concept of e-literature also feasible, and how?

SG: In many ways, the time of today is not very different from the time soon after the invention of the printing press. In those days, no one could predict how printing was going to shape the future. The same can be said about Information Technology. With its immense possibilities, no one can predict where it is going to land humans. The future appears to be both exciting and scary.

Information Technology also has the benefit of the printing press. Computer is a boon to poets and other writers. At the same time, it is a curse when it falls in wrong hands. We have to watch and wait to know what, how, and where the muscles of the genie of Information Technology are going to work.

NKA: The concept of 'Artificial Intelligence' is gaining currency. Computers are intelligent enough to perform several cognitive functions of the mind, like accounting, calculation and handling of the unmanageable data, etc. Are computers intelligent enough to create a new poem? Can a computer indulge in any creative and aesthetic activity? Can this Information Revolution create another Shakespeare? If not, is not computer deficient in something? Then, why is it so much eulogized? Your views, please.

SG: I believe that humans are the only creatures that have the faculty of thinking, called also intelligence. Computers are what they are asked to do. In spite of so much scientific progress, there is not a single software that can find grammatical errors in a sentence. Some softwares give suggestions in a limited way. There is no computer that can write a novel or a book of history. Literature is the product of creative thinking. Computers are okay for calculations and accounting, because they are fed into the computer by humans. Computers can never take the place of human intelligence. They have and will simplify life further in many ways, but humans will have to pay a price for that. Nothing is free, except for the elements of nature like air, water and the sun, though humans are taxing them now.

NKA: You are aware of both India and Pakistan. What is the solution of Indo-Pak conflict? Can novels like *A Train to Pakistan* by Khushwant Singh and *A Bend in the Ganges* by Manohar Malgonkar create symptoms of human sympathy in the hearts of the people for the persons of neighboring nation? Can communication among the literary artists across the border check the violence on the border? Please enlighten.

SG: Writers throughout the history of humankind have been trying to promote peace and to speak against injustice and oppression. We know that Lorca and Byron gave their lives in the cause of liberation. Even nowadays, we have several writers as prisoners in many countries of the world. The PEN, an international association of writers, has been trying hard to get their release. In several cases it has succeeded.

These events tend to prove that written words have a strong impact on people. This is the reason why books are banned and the writers imprisoned. In olden days, *the Vedas* in India were not within the reach of everyone. So was the case with *the Bible* in the West. Recently, the Pentagon papers concerning the Vietnam War changed the way of thinking of several Americans. Before that, the civil war for the liberation of the slaves was partly caused by a book titled *Uncle Tom's Cabin* by Harriet Beecher Stowe. In social and political fields, the writers who reflect the spirit of their ages are still remembered and read. The French and Russian revolutions were largely due to their writers. Maxim Gorky is known today for his social realism.

Shakespeare was right when he said the pen is mightier than the sword, and so was Shelley who said poets are the unacknowledged legislators of the world. Writers and poets have been behind many world revolutions. Their help has been sought in every era and in every corner of the globe. They are not silent even today — they are promoting world peace in their own way.

Writers and poets can influence people because they are involved with every aspect of life these days. They are involved with newspapers, radio and TV; they write novels, stories and articles, and write speeches for business executives and politicians. It is hard to think of even a single corner of modern life where writers are not involved in one way or another. Consequently, they are in a strong position to educate their readers, although this may be a slow process.

To promote world peace and to condemn war, I have edited two volumes of an anthology, titled *Anti-War Poems*. This anthology expresses the hopes, the dreams, the fears and frustrations of poets. Part one was released in 1984 by Vesta Publications Limited. I did not realise the result would be so encouraging when I started spreading the gospel of the anthology. News media turned out to be extremely cooperative beyond my imagination.

A poet cannot live in an ivory tower forever. If Shakespeare is alive today, it is because he has also produced in his plays the social, political, economic, moral and scientific ideas of his times. He has proved that a literature that does not reflect the spirits of the time cannot be great and of lasting nature. Even in *Paradise Lost*, which is timeless, John Milton expresses the moral controversies of the Protestants and the Roman Catholics that plagued their time and sent a British king to the gallows.

Today, the world is torn asunder with fear and hatred. There is still a grave danger of another world war, which may annihilate entire civilisation. There is a need for harmony and oneness of humankind. True writers cannot turn their backs to this reality, like the Lady of Shallot. It is very encouraging that several groups have been providing a platform of peace and I am sure that poets and writers will continue providing leadership and a climate for the further growth of peace and harmony.

NKA: According to certain scholars, literature is a social document. It is influenced by contemporary social, political, historical and religious ideals. Whereas another group of critics is of the belief that literature should have no propaganda. They believe in 'art for art's sake' theory. What, in your opinion, is the best path? In which category will you classify your writings and why? Or, is there any 'middle path'?

SG: Whether one believes in art for art's sake or propaganda, literature can not escape the social and political climate of the time. I am also a product of my time when India was divided in 1947. Those situations have left a mark on my soul that I cannot wash away no matter what kind of soap I use. John Milton is also product of his age and so was William Shakespeare before him.

Literature that is just for propaganda is not good literature. When readers read a poem, they expect aesthetic beauty, not knowledge. For knowledge, readers will go to those types of books. Art is beauty and it should not be mixed with anything else.

However, an artist needs a subject, like potters who need clay to make their pots. I use the clay of peace to make the pot of a poem. An ideal work is the right combination of the subject and the form. For an artist, art should be the first consideration. It is like a carpenter. His first job is to make a beautiful chair. He uses the wood for his material. With his tools he makes the best possible use of his material. That is what a poet is supposed to do.

As far as my work is concerned, I will leave that to critics and readers to evaluate. I do my best as a poet.

14

The Power of the Written Word: A Note on the Poetry of Stephen Gill

—P. Raja

Once a visitor from a far off country walked into the durbar hall of Bahauddin Shah and said: "Allow me to sit in your durbar and let me listen to your lecture. Reading can never be a substitute for hearing."

"Alas!" said Bahauddin, "If you are not deaf, it is sad that I should have had to wait so long to welcome you here. You see, I never give any lectures nowadays."

The visitor expressed his curiosity to know why.

Bahauddin said: "Ever since a group of partially deaf people came to see me I have stopped giving lectures. You want to know why! I said 'Do not be like a dog or a swine...' After they left me they fell out disputing as to whether I had said, 'Be a dog...' or even 'Eat swine's flesh....' With the written word this is not possible. If you are blind, someone can always read out to you."

This anecdote illustrates the power of the written word. There can be no substitute for writing. May be this is the reason why Sir Francis Bacon, the Elizabethan essayist, remarked thus: "Reading maketh a full man; conference a ready man; and writing an exact man...."

Down the history of the world, we have come across orators, poets and writers. It is always the poets who ruled the roost. We have heard of court poets. We have heard of poet laureates. But have we heard of court writers or orators? Such was the coveted honour given to poets for it is the genuine poets who speak from the heart and every poem they write is a tête-à-tête to his reader. But it is the reader who out of love for the genuine poets spreads the glory of the poets.

Plato might have been envious of the creativity of poets when he spoke for the dismissal of poets from his Republic. Cinna, the poet, might have been chased by the unruly mob in Shakespeare's play *Julius Caesar* all the time shouting "Kill him for his bad verses." Yet any number of instances can be quoted from the classic Tamil literature regarding the affinity of the royalty and nobility with the poets. The best example would be the hospitality and affection Mosi Keeranar, the poet, enjoyed in the court of a Tamil king. The poet after a tedious journey was made to wait in the court of the king when the latter was returning home after a victorious battle. The tired poet found an unoccupied cot and slept on it. But he didn't in the least know that the cot was the seat of a huge war drum. The king came home with fun and fanfare. But he was shocked to see someone sleeping on the cot meant for the royal war drum. Without any second thought he pulled out his sword and rushed towards the sleeper. The glow on the sleeping poet's face stopped him and he exclaimed: "Oh! It is our Mosi Keeranar, the poet." He pushed his sword back into the scabbard and asked for a handfan. The king began to fan the poet so that the latter could sleep in peace. Such was the love the kings had for the poets. They blessed the poets with honours and made them live an undisturbed life so that they could write their verses undisturbed.

What is it that makes the government shower encomiums and honours on poets? It is the poets' social concern, their love for their country, their affection for their fellow brethren and their sincerity to the work they do. His duty is to look for many different kinds of meanings than the ones a man finds relevant in his day-to-day life. He has to explore imaginatively forbidden areas and question the codes which govern our day-to-day lives. He has to accept that fantasies and dreams, which are denied reality in ordinary life. He has to be prepared in his world of imagination to wallow in self-pity, commit all kinds of sins, and constantly try to be somebody who he is not. It is this dual personality in every poet that immortalises the man who writes poetry.

Every poet is a creator. Every creator is akin to God, the Great Creator. And it is this creativity that carves him a niche in the mind and heart of the readers. Stephen Gill is a poet with as distinct and personal a rhythm as theirs.

When Stephen Gill was honoured with the Laurel Leaf, inscribed Laureate Man of Letters, at the 13th World Congress of Poets, held at the Pointe in Phoenix, Arizona, USA, in August 1992, the President of the United Poets Laureate International, Dr. Benjamin Yuzon, commended Gill for his books, over twenty, connected with world peace in one way or another and also for his work with many organisations for global harmony. And in his acceptance speech Stephen Gill declared that he does not write for medals and diplomas. He writes to share his feelings and experience with others. His best reward is when he succeeds in imparting his message and sharing his self with others.

It is this "sharing his self with others" that forms truly the hallmark of a poet. In his admirable poem titled "Song of a New Canadian", Stephen Gill writes:

My Canada
in thy lap
lie all nations;
humans and beasts
melt into one shape
in thy lap.

Thy land and life
and springs,
thy summer and fall
and skies
and joyful birds –
delight-giving sights –
breathe a new life in me.

A nation so great
diverse and brave
thy rivers and lakes
wide and long highways
reveal thy riches to me.
My Canada!

Thy soul
a unique temple
for every creed
for every breed.
My heart will sing
always for thee;
my lips will chant
night and day for thee.

O Canada!
My well of love

full for thee.
a peace-adoring dove!
never my love
shall cease for thee.

Even a cursory reading of this poem written to commemorate the 125th birthday of Canada is bound to catapult us to a quiver of questions that goad us to explore the historical background of the poet.

All such questions get answered in what Stephen Gill wrote as "Preface" to his poems of social concern titled *Shrine* (1999). The Preface reads like a thriller, and every gruesome incident narrated therein refuses to wriggle out of our memory. Stephen Gill, a teenager from Karol Bagh, New Delhi, had had to find a way out of that loveable place turned murderous after the partition in 1947. It was Ethiopia that gave him the comfort and the safety he needed. "But I wanted to be a writer and for that I planned to settle in an English-speaking country. I felt I needed further education." And so he applied for admission to a doctoral programme. Canada seemed to be the ideal place because the University of Ottawa offered him a part-time job and hope for a fellowship after a year.

"In Canada," writes Stephen Gill, "there are opportunities for everyone. Here, the government has given and is still giving financial help to Moslems to build their mosques; to Hindus to build their temples; and to Sikhs to build their Gurduwaras. That is what the countries of India, Pakistan and Bangladesh and other nations should be doing for minorities. Happy minorities will contribute towards the building of the nation. If minorities feel secure, they will do everything to feel proud of their heritage. Absence of security and harmony leads to econo/political disaster that endangers the stability of the majority. Protection of minorities is in the interest of the majority and whole nation even the world....Canada is the best example of co-existence of a society of diverse cultures and faiths."

While continuing to glorify Canada in fitting terms, Stephen Gill writes: "Canada is a United Nation in microcosm. It is a country where it is illegal to propagate hatred against other beliefs. It is a country where the government legally supports multi-culturalism to foster tolerance. The experience of violence, the multicultural aspect of Canada, my travels, the life of Jesus, and world federalism, in addition to George Bernard Shaw and H.G. Wells, must have nourished the plant of my outlook and the literature I am producing. I find the environment of Canada stimulating for the further nourishment of this plant."

And now one can re-read the poem quoted above in full. The background information may enhance one's appreciation and enjoyment of the poem. It was only in Canada Stephen Gill found hope in the truth that revenge does not help anyone and that violence has never solved problems in human history. Since he found out that the sharks of discrimination are everywhere, he began to write and give talks to tear the mask of ignorance and to promote non-violence. The thought of cruelty of humans always remained in his mind like his own shadow. The more he thought of it, the more he became obsessed to write about it. It is this obsession that served as midwife for the birth of his poems.

In fact, it was Canada, the country he loves and adores, that was responsible in realising himself. There was absolutely no pressure from outside to cow down as in India and no sleepless nights when he had dreams of being chased and shot at as in Ethiopia. In Canada, Stephen Gill is a different "ME":

Today
I want to be me;
I wish to sing my own song!
I want to say
something about myself.
Let me live
some of my own life—
the life of silent pains.

I want to ask
how I am.
Let me find me –
my smiles
my own hurts.

Today
Let me emerge alone
and look into me.
In the fire of self
let me radiate.

Other lyrics are also good,
but today
I want to hear me.
Let me breathe
Within my own shell.

I want to express my self
drink my own water
flow in my own way
live in me.

I want to be
my own rajah –
my own devotee.
I want to be shut
within me.

It is this freedom to be himself that gives the poet in Stephen Gill a free mind and thereby a free expression. He, being an apostle, wants his poetry to be understood. Like the eminent Tamil bard Mahakavi Subramania Bharati, Dr. Stephen Gill too writes in a simple language so that he could drive his thoughts home. Simple, sensuous, appealing and alluring are some of the adjectives one can use in the appreciation of his poetry.

Stephen Gill believes in unconditional love and global peace through a democratically elected world government. He is certainly a citizen of the world, a trait that is obvious from his poems.

To wind up one can do no better than quote in full the very first poem titled "Poet's Prayer" from his lovely collection *Songs for Harmony* (1993) that sums up in a few lines his poetic credo:

O Master:
Raise the crops of my pen
into nutrients.
Water them from the sacred font
to sustain their freshness
and vitality; the combination
of all heavenly hues.

Let them be food for thought
For every reader.
Refine them in Your smithy
To turn into
distinguished objects
for the cultured court of critics.

Display in them
Your will;
fuse them with Your beauty.
Strengthen them with manna;
array them like the rainbow.

15

Rainbow Strings: Hope in the Poetry of Dr. Stephen Gill

—Ann Iverson

The poetry of Dr. Stephen Gill summons us to the threshold of peace, to the pathway of solitude, and to the river of imagination. He offers that "The world of poetry / is woven with rainbow strings / sorted in the secret caves of desire...." And it is only in reading the lyrical lines of his work that one can feel the hope that carries us to a new belief in poetry and a new thirst for peace.

In "The World of Poetry" Gill ordains the art as "[a] sky...studded with diamonds, excavated from the rocky valley of human experience." In this line, the poem itself is given glorious healing capabilities as it lets us rise from a rocky terrain to a sky shining and faceted. His constant tone of gratitude and amazement amidst pain and suffering offers an oracle of hope that every human can and should enter. His words commit us to a new notion of believing for the good of things.

"I am often greeted / by the bursting flutters of the dove /while rambling the rayless resort/ of the fears / from the scamps of my surroundings." — This opening line from "Flight of the Dove" signifies the poet's commitment to searching for the virtuosity of hope and peace within any human struggle. In his extraordinary poem "Seeking the Dove of Peace" he continues to pull us down the path of peace with his graceful, steady lines of friendship: "Let us walk / side by side / my friend / to seek out that dove." With a language and tone filled with such trust, how could we not follow? "Let us ask all beings / even the beasts / if they would / give us their hands." So even the creatures of the world will not be left behind on the journey in search of the dove of peace.

And Gill maintains his faith in the natural world of animals and nature in his shockingly beautiful poem "Who Shall Buy" in which he offers us a resting place filled with gratitude and an over abundance of song and hope, a trust and strength in those things we take for granted.

"Who Shall Buy"

No one can buy
nor sell
the blessings of the skies
the warmth of the valleys.

No one can buy
nor sell
the freedom of the winds
the grace of the lakes
the dignity of the palm trees
the mystery of the oceans
the sobriety of the jungles
and the songs of the seasons.

No one can buy
nor sell
the fragrance of the flowers
which is a friend of the universe;
and the inter-dependence
of all animals, nations and nature
who form a family with humans
and who breathe
the same air
under the same canopy.

While Dr. Gill's poetry travels many diverse topics including war, abuse, death, and disease, he always returns to the dove of peace, the god of harmony, the voice of oneness, the rainbow strings. His art extends to us a new vision of nobility and calls us to gaze upon the face of hope and peace.

16

Stephen Gill: Poet and Protester for Peace

—John Paul Loucky

If a literary award were combined with a Nobel Peace Prize, Stephen Gill would surely be recommended for it. His writings span poetic works on many topics, a majority of them sprinkled abundantly with non-violent, pro-peace themes. In addition, his prose essays delineate the urgent need for protecting the human rights of all.

As a Pakistani believer now residing in Canada, Gill writes from first-hand experience and detailed knowledge of how the rights of minorities, especially those of women and non-Muslims, have been systematically suppressed for years by unjust laws in his country of origin. In such countries extreme religious ideologies have often been allowed to control so much of society that legal, political, educational and economic rights and opportunities are prevented from flowering freely.

Gill's writings provide a much-needed moral compass and social conscience for the world in an age torn by violent fanaticisms and unjust, prejudicial ideologies. They cover such glaring topics as kidnappings, rapes and forced conversions of innocent Hindus and Christians by radical groups and other abuses of power by those who want their majority numbers to rule, instead of allowing reason, fairness, law and conscience to reign.

On peace, Gill has collected and edited two anthologies of anti-war poems. One cannot read these, especially in this Age of Terror, without often wincing at the terrible cost of violence, at the dreadful price of victory, and at the extravagant cost of freedom. Gill's own incisive and insightful poems on this ever-present theme show us his own heart-beat for world justice and equality. They include such works as *The Dove of Peace* and *Songs for Harmony*, as well as *Shrine: Poems of Social Concerns*.

Many published articles about Stephen Gill and his poems and books have been collected into a work called *Glimpses* (1999). Its contents include interviews and works about the writer's background, reviews and critical studies of his works, divided into sections on his Fiction, Poetry and Poetry Anthologies. Other eulogies to his writings and work for peace are included in its Addendum. It may be the best overall commentary about his extensive works. Speaking there of his own poems, Gill states his overall aim: "I have tried to catch the flame of love in a net of diverse techniques and forms ... with a view to escape the monotony of the beaten track." This he does admirably well.

Two notable comments about Gill's *Shrine: Poems of Social Concerns* (1999) that bear repeating are these: "Dr. Stephen Gill, a poet, critic and novelist, is an Indian settled in Canada. He is a recipient of several poetry awards. He has authored 25 books to date. His poetry and prose have been published in more than 500 publications around the world. Peace is his major area of interest" (Chambial, *Glimpses,* p.190). Having experienced the terrible horrors of racial and religious killings in India before its partition, Gill has become a "sensitive humanitarian who longs and prays for the elimination of man's hatred for man from man's heart, and the realisation of a new heaven on earth where human beings remain only human and humane purged of all devilish attributes" (Ibid.).

A second commentary from these *Glimpses* is that of Chote Lal Khatri, who stated:

> What is remarkable about Gill is that he writes verse or prose with a mission to bring peace, harmony and brotherhood. As he writes in the Preface "The cure to the malady of religious and racial fanaticism and violence lies in the acceptance of the values of tolerance, understanding and co-existence." This mission has become a passion for him that keeps reverberating in his writings and speeches. In this respect, his poetry may be called a vehicle in aid to his crusades for world peace. But he cannot be called a propagandist. For he is propagating nothing of his own but trying to spread and consolidate the most cherished values of humanity which are universal. (188)

Although the poet admires Canada as a United Nations in microcosm, his overly high hopes placed in federalism and in human nature may be easily questioned by looking at the incredibly fallen nature of man, continuous crime, war and violence throughout history, and at the repeated failures of the UN to solve problems like Rwanda, Iraq, and the Arab-Israeli conflict, to name but a few. Nevertheless, "Hope springs eternal in the human breast." May it ever be so, but may it never be misplaced. Perhaps it is more fitting in the face of so many intractable world problems and conflicts to recall and compare these with the Psalmist's hope that "Some trust in chariots and some in horses [and some in WMDs and nuclear bombs], but we will remember the name of the Lord our God." Who else can change human nature or rescue it from its degenerating path on this "Eve of Destruction," as the song and poem ask?

17

Poet Stephen Gill: A Dreamer of Peace

—Aju Mukhopadhyay

Poets are often dreamers. No wonder that Stephen Gill, born at Sialkot, Punjab, in undivided India, who spent his innocent childhood days with nightmarish experiences during the turbulent communal disharmony in New Delhi, who has ever been concerned about the sordid human nature all around us, about the ever failing human attempt to achieve peace, would remain a dreamer throughout his life.

During his teens Stephen lived in Karol Bagh, New Delhi, which was then torn between marauding communalists, where riot, arson, loot, rape and killing were the orders of the days, not mainly because of religious bigotry, for that was not the immediate cause, but for the rage of communal fury systematically aroused in them by the so-called cunning rulers who followed the grand policy of *divide and rule* for years. Not only in the capital was the fire raging, it was almost everywhere. specially in the border areas like Punjab and Bengal. What the poet experienced in his childhood in 1947 was a minor part of the mammoth of communal disharmony in all aspects of life. The most virulent type of arson, rape, riot, killing and other cruelties of goons with silent or supportive police inaction was enacted earlier in the great Direct Action Day on 16 August, 1946 in Calcutta. The leaders were bewildered, helpless and hopeless; they wished for the partition only to rule in divided States.

However, the history is very long and disputed, at least by the historians, as to who played what role during those days.

"This is the realm or condition of the 'dead people', those who have rejected spiritual values by yielding to bestial appetites or violence, or by perverting their human intellect to fraud or malice against their fellow men. As subject matter it is the lowest, ugliest, most materialistic of the whole poem", wrote Archibald T. Mac Allister in his introduction to the *Inferno*, the first part of the immortal poem, *The Divine Comedy*, by Dante Alighieri.

It was a living inferno around him. In the prefaces to his two adored books of poems, *Shrine* (1999) and *Songs before Shrine* (2007), Stephen Gill has reported his childhood experiences of the riot- torn New Delhi at length which to a great extent became the basis of his poetic expression and the cause for his Peace Project. So important incidents and experiences, which formed the material foundation of his *Shrine*, need some elaboration.

> The anticipation of danger lurking in the air all the time killed me piece by piece with the unseen sword of the distress of my mind. (17)
>
> My trust in humanity was shaken so badly in those days that I had to struggle with myself patiently for a long time to recover it. (14)

To flee from the choking condition he got a job after frantic efforts in Ethiopia and left the country for it. After sometime he shifted to England and then to Canada after securing a part-time job with prospects of further studies.

> In Ethiopia, as in India, I had dreams of being chased and soldiers shooting people for no reason, while I was trying to escape. I had difficulty in falling asleep that afflicted my life from the days of the riots. Those nightmares followed me in Canada. (18)

In Canada, "for the first time I found pride and freedom in the expression of my beliefs openly." (24)

Besides some well-known personalities like Jesus Christ, H.G. Wells and George Bernard Shaw, the cultural atmosphere of Canada "nourished the plant of my outlook and the literature I am producing." (26) wrote the poet. Praising Canada he said, "Canada is the best example of co-existence of a society of diverse cultures and faiths" (25).

Through the preface we know that he wished to remain in the community of Christians for safety but his father did not feel alike. We also come to know of the poet's disappointment when he realised that being a Christian would not automatically attract the help of his fellow religionists, and that in fact they were never a target of the warring groups. So fear only consumed him. No life-threatening attempt was made on his family. Though the poet has not been nostalgic about his birthplace or the religion of the country he was born in he has literary links galore with it. In the context of his condemnation about the happenings in India around 1947, one has to consider certain facts which affected India for centuries. Incidents of 1947 were the cumulative effect of such happenings.

It is to be remembered that for more than thousand years this country was looted and ravished by barbaric forces coming from across the borders. It is to be remembered that Hinduism is not an abode of polytheism only but of monotheism too, that the *Vedas* taught the world everything about the essence of the divine before few recorded religions showing any sign of sublime spiritual identity of God, that in spite of diverse faiths Indians were culturally united throughout the ages, yet accepted all other incoming people and their faiths to coexist in their country, that large numbers of Indian people were converted, forcibly or otherwise by other religions and rulers, that it is India and its people who in spite of all onslaught of barbaric waves have not vanished like in many Western countries, rather absorbed all other cultures in its body and has been progressing to stand almost equal to any other culture and civilisation. No Indian calls people of other faiths infidels or idolaters though worshipping a man's image or name too is idolatry. In the integral culture of India all other cultures and peoples are included. India waits with her spiritual gift for the world to lead it tc perfection in future, as envisioned by Sri Aurobindo and the Mother.

The poet writes in the same preface of *Shrine*, "It is still an enigma for me how people who appear to be normal in their everyday life turn into animals in the name of their religious creed. Is it from Satan or in the blood?"

It may be answered that it happens when religion in its lower strata divides. It is the same strata which forces and allures people to convert from their own religion to the others so that the converted enlarge the body of the other religion. It is the voice of Satan which says that one religion or one faith is at the pinnacle of man's spiritual flight, only one person acts as the savior of the mankind. And somewhere the Satan asserts that anybody who does not believe its creed is infidel, he should be punished. Not all the scriptures tell the same thing. At the higher level religion becomes a worship of the white spirit, the absolute. In it there is no division, no tendency to proselytise. The tendency to proselytise is the ill gotten child of the religion at its lower strata.

Partition stories have been written in some books. Remarkable among them are *Tamas* by Bhishma Sahani, *Train to Pakistan* by Khushwant Singh and *Freedom at Midnight* by Dominique Lapierre and Larry Collins.

It may be said that the disastrous partition could be avoided in 1942 when Sir Strafford Cripps offered Dominion Status which at first was accepted by Nehru and C. Rajagopalachari but rejected by Gandhi. Sri Aurobindo sent his personal messenger to the then leaders advising to accept it. Instead, Quit India movement was begun which proved to be full of violence and the truncated freedom came as it would voluntarily come, under the helpless condition of the British. It was the example of another Himalayan blunder of Gandhiji.

The ill feeling continues, illustrated by the post-Godhra incidents in Gujarat in 2002, widely publicised by the media though we are not yet clear about the Godhra incidents. The macabre incidents continue to happen in Bangladesh from time to time ever since the first partition and their independence with Indian help in 1971 and beyond. There is hardly any writer or medium to tell us the actual position except one Taslima Nasrin telling us the facts in such work as her novel, *Lajja*, for fear of being marked as non-progressive. The exodus of Bangladeshi people, actually Indians, continue from their motherland on the ground that the majority were converted to another religion gradually, now forming the majority of the population there. It is a shame that such work based on facts has been marked as un-Islamic by the fundamentalists. The Bangladeshi writer is being hounded in Free India.

Stephen Gill is highly conscious of all such incidents of terror throughout the world including in Somalia, Bosnia, Rwanda and Lebanon. His heart bleeds with the bleeding of the tortured people of Asia and Africa. He has become very sensitive to such incidents whereby man loses the right to freedom and honour of life. His poems are replete with his heart's pouring of sympathy for the poor and the down-trodden. His childhood memories are rife in his poems:

> In the lap of
> unruffled solitude
> I hold the book of memories. . . .

open my inner eyes
to the fruits
of pains and pleasures. ("Journey")

I have planted in my yard
the trees
which give the fruits of pain,
tear, loneliness
and self destruction. ("Legacy")

He finds devastation all around:

Bodies rotting in ditches
or dumped with the garbage.
Bodies washing up
onto the beaches. . .
All lie here
like the mowed grass on the lawn.
Who are these faces
on whose eyes and cheeks
drops of blood
glitter like pearls. ("A Familiar Scene")

I have gazed
into the graveyard of their eyes. . .
In the furnace
of their helplessness
they burn themselves . . . ("Refugees")

Like a master social worker and sympathetic psychiatrist he finds out in "Slavery", "A Heroin Addict", "Abandoned" and "Amputee" the reasons why a person becomes a murderer, another a drug addict, a boy devil and an innocent girl worse than a harlot. For example, mark the following expressions:

He comes from a home
where
neglect and desertion
were common. ("Abandoned")

The years of abuse
has damaged the delicate nerves
of her relationship with God,
men and herself. . .
Scenes of childhood lock her
behind the barbed wires
of her fragile hopes. ("Amputee")

Though he has immense hope from Democracy, he finds it maimed as autocrats rule the roost. Muscle is more powerful than sane voice of wisdom, as we find in "Lotus of Freedom", "Seed of Democracy" and "The Ballot has Muscles." In the poem "Who Runs Our World", Gill shows that politics, money and blood run our world.

With a sympathetic heart, social concern and unending inquisitiveness the poet finds hopelessness as the presiding deity of the time:

> Year after year
> the same concerns.
> Life comes back to life. . .
> The future seems crumbling
> in a fog of sands. ("Year after Year")

Every year the same act is repeated:

> Only calendars become new.
> Some cards are traded
> some feasts are arranged.
> This is not a change. ("On the New Year")

> In this valley of sand
> not all that we see is true:
> only the gossip. ("A New Canadian in Toronto")

Science, technology and commerce have done miracles in the material world but have not helped mankind's elevation to any higher plane of life:

> I am the father of conflicts,
> engulfed by the devils of technology. . . .
> Dreams open their windows
> to let in the breeze of repose
> but the hands of commerce
> frustrate their attempts
> by polluting surroundings
> with the acid rains
> of rush. . . rush. . . rush. ("Twentieth Century Says")

The poet's hope, it seems, has been crushed:

> It is easier to carve a god
> out of stone
> than to curve a being
> out of human. ("In My Books")

But he has hopes in the will of masses:

Like a thunder
I fuse into the clouds.
When I drop
even the earth yields.
Cruelty cannot kill me. ("Will of Masses")

The poet often speaks biographically:

The immigrant in me
talks of the days. . . .
Those painful shrieks
hidden in his blood
stagger at night. . . .
The Canadian in me
works harder day after day
to pay his bills
hoping one day
he would be free. ("Tenants in Me")

But the poet is quite sure to stay on in his country of refuge, where he has found comparative peace and security. He refutes the charge that he is an intruder for he knows that exodus and resettlement are part of the human routine throughout the history. Have not the Whites settled in new-found lands driving out the original inhabitants? If he is asked to go back,

Where would the whites go?
How about Mohawks and Inuit?
If you know Canadian history! . . .
Do not tell me to go anywhere,
my friend.
This is our land
where our father lives.
We are all in exile. ("Go Back")

Saying this he adds,

. . . the world has become a village
where no one is an island to self
any more
any more. (ibid.)

Some of the autobiographical poems are quite intimate where the poet looks at himself in retrospect:

> Under
> the brow of the cloudy skies
> those deep eyes
> dropped the dew of innocence
> on the wings of my guilt
> which I carry still
> while searching for Me. ("A Handshake")

In a similar poem we find the faint echo of romantic love, as if with himself again:

> Whenever I think of you
> lightning thunders
> in the lonesomeness of my retreat. ("Peace of Mind")

"Poetry is to present my vision and my concerns, and to conceive peace in a peaceful way. The compelling influence of my crusade is peace that is beauty; the peace that is creative, the peace that makes life meaningful," the poet writes in the preface to *Song Before Shrine* but it ever eludes him:

> For a long time
> I have been hearing
> the dove of peace will be freed
> shortly. . .
> progress has been made. . . .
> our homes now better adorned
> with thorns of hatred
> a few more nuclear bombs
> remains to be developed
> and contested
> man is to breathe his last
> in the smoke. . . ("The Dove of Peace")

Earlier in the *Shrine* he wrote:

> Our rulers talk of peace
> but it is futile
> when nuclear powered marines
> sail over breasts of the oceans;
> missiles look down like hawks

and neutrons
make fun of every life. ("Talking of Peace")

It seems really a fun to seek peace here. What he witnessed and experienced, kept such an indelible mark on the pages of his memory that he never forgets them. In "I Have Seen" he writes about his experiences about all sorts of human failings, treachery, debauchery and infidelity. He remembers,

Famished walking skeletons
bodies resting unshrouded
forlorn infants and old
sad sighs of the sisters. ("I have Seen")

Even

In many aspects
mosquitoes excel humans.
They are happy sea-waves
also honest and brave. ("Ode to Mosquitoes")

A child ever wails to get new things and remains ever hankering after new desires, so the poet finds,

It is man's fate
to chase pleasure
as do toddlers. ("Man is Ever a Child")

Peace is an enigmatic being to him:

You're a will-o'-the-wisp
a chain of onion layers
mysterious, another paradox
you seem cruel and flippant
or just an image to believe. ("Harmony and Peace")

Beyond those solitary church towers
I see the sun of harmony sinking...
("Evening of Harmony")

The sinking sun shines close by
while empty stomachs hold the mast.
No Christ
Appears to appease the savage sea.
("Rays of Harmony")

We remember, Sri Aurobindo said that all problems of life are essentially problems of harmony. The poet here feels that harmony has gone,

> . . . night of terror
> chews peace
> in the endless depth
> of cultural insanities. ("Evening of Harmony")

Not only human discordance, environmental pollutants also choke him. He wishes to hibernate,

> Away from swarming cities
> Stench from pollutants. . . .
> 'where waves no longer roar
> distrust has no teeth. ("Let us Hibernate")

He seeks Nirvana in silence where drops of harmony produce a lullaby (Nirvana):

> I wish to breathe undisturbed
> away from obnoxious sights. . .
> and dusty pride in the march
> of technology and science. ("In My Own Womb")

He wishes, as a remedy, to invoke the blessings of the sages. Aren't they Indian sages?

> . . . those sages could teach
> scheming players
> how to love and live! ("Where are They?")

After a long journey with the poet through his poems, do we not feel that peace evades him? Apparently he is frustrated but the poet in him never dies for ultimately he is a seer, ever dreamer of peace. He beseeches Nightingales, Clouds, Dove, Butterfly, Eagle and the Angel to bestow him their special faculties to help him feel 'the flesh of peace.' ("If You Lend Me")

In "Idol for My Temple", a nice poem like many of his, he wishes to borrow vibrations from different aspects of nature to weave the pattern of peace. Wishing, inviting and praying finally gives place to dreaming:

The rays of his presence
shall unlock the portals
of human castles
to defeat demons.
Prince is the coming age. ("Prince of Peace")

The pulsation of my heart
mumbles to me
that the adders of today
would pave the way
for that glorious dawn
when even thorns and beasts
brighten their faces and eyes
in the panoramic landscape
of harmony. ("Domain of Peace")

Here we hear a distant echo of the hope for the possibility of a Life Divine on earth as envisioned by Sri Aurobindo, one of the greatest poets and philosophers of the world, in his *The Life Divine* and the largest spiritual epic poem in English language, *Savitri.*

Sri Aurobindo and after him the Mother, his collaborator, caused the descent and emergence of eternal Supramental (a term coined by Sri Aurobindo, meaning the highest spiritual consciousness so far envisaged) light, force and consciousness on earth through integral yoga. They said that gradually, as mankind would be soaked in that consciousness, all discord, disharmony, hatred, competition and inequality would vanish and a life divine shall be established on earth. These hopes are not futile. They will be real and concrete if we collaborate. In his long poem, *The Flame*, Stephen Gill prays for the deliverance from the ugly disharmony and terrorism. He prays to the divine:

To direct my steps
towards the shores of the pure bliss
of your peace
I shall dip in the esoteric stream
that meanders along the woodlands
of my absolute fidelity.

As a pcet Stephen Gill has discussed 'What is poetry?' in his introduction to books of poems and in interviews, with reference to his own experiences. As a lover of freedom from all traditions and customs in writing poems, for which Japanese medium is the best, he feels that he has poured in his ideas about it in the introduction to *Flashes*, a collection of Haiku.

Let us now enter into his theory of poetry. If we take Wordsworth's definition of poetry, 'Overflow of powerful feelings' as emotion in contrast to T.S. Eliot's definition of it as 'An escape from emotions', we come to Coleridge's 'Emotions recollected in tranquillity'. Though none of these definitions is liked by Gill exactly, he comes round to the central point of emotion which he names as 'airy beings' to be caught in the net of poet's words. Here he gives poetic talent only 25 per cent credit, rest being given to his labour for selecting words, correcting and polishing, etc. Though he has said by way of reference that poetry is spiritual and psychic experience, he has not dwelt in it much. It is the domain of a yogi-poet, as Sri Aurobindo was, who gave much value to intuitive faculty of a poet and said that there are higher sources of poetry like the Overmind and yet higher levels, mainly in his voluminous treatise, *The Future Poetry*. After some years of writing poetry, words dropped on to his pen from higher regions. He did not think to write anything during the larger part of his life.

Gill has given 75 per cent credit to labour in composing a poem but in his long discussion about Haiku he says, "I like to be free like nature itself. . . . I do not perceive much creativity in work in which a poet has to struggle to confer to the established norms."

He makes full and meaningful use of metaphors, sometimes in excess, in his poems with other ornaments and occasional rhyming; quite true and spontaneous expression of the poet. And there lies the beauty of his poems, often with apt imagery. By nature he is a poet with a sensitive heart, a creative brain and a passion for poetry.

His family migrated from their home in Sialkot, now in Pakistan, and settled in New Delhi, India. From there the poet sought shelter in Canada after a short sojourn to Ethiopia and England. The viewpoint of an immigrant always keeps him alive to his situation in life. His points of view were portrayed in his novel *Immigrant*. Such things and more he said in his reply to questions by Dr. Nilanshu Kumar Agarwal in an interview. Besides this the poet has made a long discourse on diaspora in this interview. He has made elaborate explanations about immigrants, diasporans, economic refugees and such relevant terms which are eye openers to many, though some may dispute some of his viewpoints. While these discussions are limited to theories, the actual position of first generation diaspora, the pathetic mix of culture in the second generation and its result have been aptly handled by Jhumpa Lahiri in her novel, *The Namesake*.

On the basis of his experiences from the childhood and the present socio-politico-economic conditions of the world, Gill has become peace prone. He earnestly wishes to establish a peaceful world order. Not only has he written poems urging peace but edited two volumes of anti-war anthologies of poems. "I hope that my writings about peace will cause change in the thinking of my readers", he has written. He has been writing essays in support of peace. Many poets are involved in it, like Maria Cristina Azcona of Argentina. Many believe that poets are specially positioned in the society to initiate a peace process. Peace is, according to him, absence of war or fear of war and bloodshed. But this is negative peace. In yogic parlance peace is a positive force generated in the minds and will of the people. When peace governs the heart of the people, bringing the willingness to achieve it, even at the cost of some conveniences and comforts, peace may dwell among us. The poet is variously engaged in propagating his idea of peace throughout the world through his pen and speech. He is a member and responsible office bearer of many organisations, both social and literary, both Canadian and international.

Though awards do not exactly signify the merits of a person for obvious reasons, on whom such awards are bestowed from various quarters, they may be said to have some real worth. Dr. Stephen Gill, author of more than 25 books including novel, short stories, critiques and essays, of which poetry books number nine, has been chosen by several universities, the world over, for different honours. In 2005 Ansted University, England, appointed him The Poet Laureate. In 1994 he was elected the poet of peace for 1993.

The poet is very much alive to the world situations and happenings. He often protests, as he has recently done, to the demand for Pakistan's return to democracy, arguing that there has never prevailed a real democracy. He has been constantly writing, editing and speaking through different media including internet and print media. He is a man vibrant in literature. He has been constantly working for world peace.

18

Stephen Gill: A Time-Tested Person With A Time-Trusted Vision

—Tholana Ashok Chakravarthy

Stephen Gill, Poet Laureate of Ansted University, Canada, is undoubtedly a gem among the gems and a time-tested person with a time-trusted vision. His relentless efforts and commitment to enlighten the world on the necessity of global peace and social awakening demonstrate his concern on the grave dangers of violence and war, looming large to destroy the basic fabric of civilisation. Worried over the future of mankind, in the ongoing phase where the world is caught in the mire of fear and hatred, the Poet Laureate surfaced to uplift us with the soul-stirring tunes of harmony and oneness of humankind.

Stephen Gill strongly contends that even thinkers and social reformers have talked of 'World Citizenship' for centuries and that the idea is not abstract. His theory that, one major step that would lead to world peace is control of the international anarchy through an international government, which unfolds his instinct of crusade for peace and welfare of mankind. To foster world harmony, Gill, like a lion-hearted and dedicated representative of non-violence, vies to promote world peace, build a bridge of love and understanding amongst the humans and relentlessly aims to dismantle the mood of anger and despair. By exploring the existing dangers and paving ways and means to make the world a safe heaven and 'the better' place to live in, he is instrumental in bringing together thousands of international poets and organisations to hold back the factor of hatred and violence and to knit a golden shield of universal peace. Keeping aloof all religious and geographical disparities, clamouring for peace through his steadfast and strong inspiration, organisations and poets from every corner of the globe are competing to impart Gill's thoughts and theories.

Several of Gill's poetic themes focus on universal peace, condemnation of wars and bloodshed, and surge with thought-provoking waves of concern that "despite it took millions of years to build human civilisation, a nuclear warfare can destroy us in minutes". In one of his soul-stirring poems, "The Dove Of Peace", Gill grabs the readers' indepth sprouting thoughts with the amazing lines, "For a long time I have been hearing the dove of peace will be freed shortly, and for that dove's total safety, cannons have been installed over dead bodies." He could shrewdly tune the poetic strings in such a striking way in the poem, "Isle Of Art" – "Away from the life-stifling smoke / from the heartbreak house / lies a solitary isle of art / where I have tended / a garden for my retreat .... No haste / no worry / no malice / and no darkness of prejudice lurks here. Eyes set on my horizon / on calm waves I sail here."

A recipient of several awards and conferred with three prestigious doctorates, the author of over 20 books, including fiction and collections of poems, Stephen Gill's sphere of concentration steadied on universal peace, social concerns and human rights. How deep is his association, eyeing on to foster world harmony, can be ascertained from the albums: *Aman* (peace) and *Aman ki Rah* (Road to Peace), a collection of poems in Hindu and Urdu, set to tune by renowned musicians. Born in Pakistan and brought-up in India, before finally settling in Canada, Gill is influenced by the people and cultures of both the nations. In the excerpts of Gill's interview that appeared in *The Atlantic Literary Review*, he strongly advocated the need for a 'World Government' with a punch of powerful words: "The World Government does not mean to get rid of national languages and cultures. Countries like India and Canada are already multicultural and multilingual. World citizenship is an extension of these realities and if languages and cultures can survive in these and in other nations, they can survive also under the one-world government."

A fountain of inspiration, Gill contends, true writers cannot turn their backs to reality and they should focus on the ideals of civilisation and the future of humankind. Yes, undoubtedly, the citizens of the world should be educated, enlightened and imparted about the futility of wars and the catastrophic outcome. Better late than never, the time is ripe for individuals, novelists, fiction and non-fiction writers, poets and publishers to bring to light the aspect of world unity, a vital feature to foster cultural, religious and harmonious theory for human survival. It's time to question one's own-self, why not follow the footsteps of Gill, the master-mind and a key personality who is instrumental in sowing the seeds of harmony for transforming the climate to befit universal peace and harmony.

Bibliography

Primary Sources

Poetical Works

Gill, Stephen. *Reflections.* Kytes, 1973.

-------- . *Wounds.* Vesta, 1974.

-------- . *Moans And Waves.* Vesta, 1989.

-------- . *The Flowers of Thirst.* Vesta, 1991.

-------- . *The Dove of Peace.* M.A.F. Press, 1993.

-------- . *Songs For Harmony.* Rose Shell Press, 1993.

-------- . *Divergent Shades.* Writer's Forum, 1995.

-------- . *Shrine.* World University Press, 1999.

-------- . *Flashes.* Imprint, 2007.

-------- . *Songs Before Shrine.* Authorspress, 2007.

-------- . *The Flame.* Vesta, 2008.

Fictional Works

Gill, Stephen. *Life's Vagaries.* Vesta, 1974.

-------- . *Why.* Vesta, 1977.

-------- . *The Loyalist City.* Vesta, 1979.

-------- . *Simon And The Snow King.* Vesta, 1981.

-------- . *Immigrant.* Vesta, 1982.

-------- . *The Blessings of a Bird.* Vesta, 1983.

Non-Fictional Works

Gill, Stephen. *The Discovery of Bangladesh.* Colin Venton, 1975.

-------- . *Scientific Romances of H.G. Wells.* Vesta, 1977.

-------- . *Six Symbolist Plays of Yeats.* Vesta, 1978.

--------. *Political Convictions of G.B. Shaw.* Vesta, 1980.

--------. *Sketches of India.* Vesta, 1988.

--------. *English Grammar for Beginners.* Colin Venton, 1998.

Books In Urdu, Punjabi and Hindi

Gill, Stephen. *Aman Di Ghuggi* (Poems in Punjabi language). Publishers Cooperative, 1995.

--------. *Jazeera* (Poems in Urdu). Vesta, 2005.

--------. *Jazeera* (Poems in Hindi). Vesta, 2006.

Edited Books

Gill, Stephen. *Poets of the Capital.* Borealis Press, 1973.

--------. *Seaway Valley Poets.* Vesta, 1975.

--------. *Green Snow: Anthology of Canadian Poets of Asian Origin.* Vesta, 1976.

--------. *Tales From Canada For Children Everywhere.* Vesta, 1979.

--------. *Anti-War Poems.* Vol. 1.Vesta, 1984.

--------. *Anti-War Poems.* Vol. 2.Vesta, 1986.

--------. *Vesta's Who's Who of North American Poets.* Vesta, 1990.

Works In Translation

Gill, Stephen. *Zakhmi Perchawen* (Poems in Punjabi). Trans. Mohinder Kaur Gill. Suchinton Prakashan, 1980.

--------. *Reflexions Et Blessures* (Poems in French). Trans. Roland Hamel, Vesta, 1979.

--------. *Awasi* (Punjabi Translation of his novel *Immigrant).* Trans. Balbir Momi. Pal Pocket Books, 1986.

--------. *Parwasi* (Translation of *Immigrant* in Punjabi) Trans. N. Singh and S. Sarna. Vikendrit Group of Publications, 1989.

Albums

Gill, Stephen. *Aman* (Urdu / Hindi poems performed with music by a famous singer in a cassette). Released in 2003.

--------. *Aman Ki Rah* (Urdu / Hindi poems performed with music by another famous singer from Pakistan). Released in 2005.

________________. *Selected Interviews Of Dr. Stephen Gill* (DVD album of about two hours). Released in 2005.

Website

http://www.stephengill.ca

Secondary Sources

Books

Darwesh, Hamadan. Ed. *Glimpses*. Vesta, 2005.

Hines, George. *Stephen Gill and His Works*. Authorspress, 2008.

Articles

Ahsan, Syed M. "Concept of Evil in Gill's *Shrine*", online: pakistanchristianpost.com.

Ansted University Educational Board. "Stephen Gill", *Cyber Literature* (India), Vol.9, June 2002.

Bennett, Thea. "Yeats and Reincarnation", *The Canadian India Times*, January 20, 1972.

Bhashyam, K.N. "All is not Rosy", *The Hindu,* (India), May 15, 1979.

Boland, Viga. "Book of the Month", *ByWord* (India), June 1977.

-------- ."Life's Vagaries and Wounds", *Medium*, Vol.2, March 4, 1976.

-------- . "Book of the Month (Green Snow)", *Byword* (India), July 1976.

-------- . "Discovery", *Canadian Authors & Bookman* (Canada), Fall 1976.

Carter, Alixe. "Stephen Gill: Writer, Publisher But A Doer First", *The Ottawa Journal,* October 29 1977.

Chambial, D.C. "*Songs For Harmony*", *Poetcrit* (India), July 1999.

-------- . "Stephen Gill *Shrine*", *Poetcrit* (India), January 2000.

Connell, Michelle D. "Gill's *Shrine* Implores To Think", *From Both Sides of the Ocean* (USA), September-October, 2000.

Darwesh, Hamadan. "A study of Faiz Ahmed Faiz and Stephen Gill", *Glimpses*, Vesta, 2005.

Dewar, Russ. "*Life's Vagaries*", from the introduction of *Life's Vagaries*, Vesta, 1974.

Drake, Bobbie. 'Texas Poet Visits Dr. Gill", *The India Globe,* (USA), December 1992.

Durrell, Robert. "Romances of H.G. Wells", *Temiskaming Speaker* (Canada), April 14, 1976.

-------- . "Life's Vagaries", *Temiskaming Speaker* (Canada), May 12, 1976.

-------- . "Immigrant by Stephen Gill", *Nugget Book Reviews* (Canada), February 16, 1979.

-------- . "*Why*", *Nugget Focus* (Canada), January 13, 1978.

Elliott, Bianca. "*Shrine*", *Masihi Sansar* (Punjab, India), April 15, 2001; also *Kafla International* (Chandigarh, India), Sept.-Dec. 2001.

Fleischer, Denise. "Adds Another to Collection", *Gotta Write Network* (USA), Winter 1991.

Fletcher, Peggy. "Alienation", *Canadian Author & Bookman*, Vol. 51, No. 4, summer 1976.

Gamble, Rick. "Literature Said Vital Force for World Peace", *The Expositior*, Sept. 8, 1976.

Gill, K.S. "Poems of Social Consciousness", *South Asian Diary* (Canada), November 1, 2000.

Gill, Rashid. "Dr. Stephen Gill: A Born Poet of Peace", online: *pakistanchristianpost.com*.

Green, Mary. "Hard Work Pays Off", *The Montreal Star*, (Canada), Feb. 21, 1978.

Harper, A.W.J. "Struggle for Democracy", *The London Free Press*, June 18, 1977.

Heward, Burt. "Newcomer to Canada Shows How Publishing Can Survive", *The Ottawa Citizen* (Canada), April 12, 1977.

Holt, Rochelle L. "A Call For Peace", *The Pilot*, (USA), January 20, 1992.

-------- . "Anti-War Poems", *Small Press Review* (USA), August 1985.

Keywan, Zonia. "Publisher Scorns Federal Handouts", *The Gazette, Daily* (Canada), January 20, 1979.

Khatri, Chhote Lal. "*Shrine (Poems of Social Concern)*", *Cyber Literature* (India), December 1999.

Koch, Terry. "Ideas Don't Report to Customs", *At Your Leisure*", (USA), April 9, 1978.

Lakhnavi, Prabhat Kumar Sarwar. "Peace in Sahir Ludhianvi and Stephen Gill", Online: *Asian Tribune*, *Blitz Internet Edition*, and *pakistanchristianpost*.

Leitao, Lino. "Immigrant Novel: An Understanding of Mankind", *The Asian Tribune* (Canada), August 15, 1980.

-------- . "The concept of harmony in the Ojibways of Canada and the poetry of Stephen Gill. *Seva Bharati Journal of English Studies* (India), Vol.3, February 2007.

Linder, Norma West. "A Critical Study of H.G. Wells", *The Link* (Canada), August 10, 1976.

-------- . "*Green Snow*", *Sarnia Gazette* (Canada), August 11, 1976.

Long, Virginia Love. "*Songs for Harmony*", *Poetcrit* (India), 1997.

Lynch, Peggy Zuleika. "Fly on the Wall Interview Presents Stephen Gill", *Poetry in The Arts Newsletter*, No. 23, January 2001.

Manchanda, Madan. "Love is the Eternal Passion", *The Pioneer* (India), April 4, 1996.

Mawaheb International, The. (Canada). 'Stephen Gill's 1999 Literary Tour to India", April 1999.

Pakistan Christian Post. "An Evening With Dr. Stephen Gill", online: pakistanchristianpost.com.

Parakot, Manjula. "Interesting Indians", The *Canadian India Times* (Canada), November 18, 1978.

Parameswari, D. "The Cultural Baggage: A Reading of Stephen Gill's *Immigrant*", online: *pakistanchristianpost.com*.

Penny, Margaret. "Time is True Test for Writer's Ability", *The Standard-Freeholder,* October 19, 1975.

Phillips, Bluebell S. "Gill Side Stepped My Two-Step", *Asian Tribune* (Canada).

-------- . "Two Novels of Gill", *The Asian Tribune* (Canada), October, 1979.

-------- . "Wounds", *The Canadian India Times,* (Canada) September 19, 1974.

Preddie, Calvin. "Scholarly Work on Yeats", *The Standard-Freeholder* (Canada), February 10, 1972.

Prime, Patricia. "*Shrine: Poems of Social Concerns*", *Mawaheb International* (Canada), June 2000.

Raphael, Maryanne. "Gill's Poetry Enriches Life", *Bridge-in-Making* (India), January-April, 1998.

Rasha, Miter. "A Multidimensional Person", *Perdesi Panjab* (Canada), February 16, 1979.

Reyes, Sophia. "A Hindu's Journey to Christian Faith", *The Daily Standard-Freeholder,* (Canada), July 23, 1994.

Sahu, Antaryami. "Stephen Gill: A Poet of Peace and Harmony", *Bharat Times* (Canada), March 2004.

Samal, S. "Eros in Gill's The Flowers of Thirst", *Writer's Lifeline* (Canada), 1992, No.3.

-------- . "*Shrine*", *Replica* (India), January-March, 2000.

-------- . "Stephen Gill's Immaculate Articles", *Kafla International* (India), No. 20, Sept., Dec. 1998.

Sarangi, Jaydeep. "Interview with Stephen Gill", *The Atlantic Literary Review,* (India), Vol. 5, Nos. 3-4, July-Sep. & Oct.-Dec., 2004.

-------- . "Land and Identity in the Poetry of Stephen Gill & Jayanta Mahapatra", online: *pakistanchristianpost.com.*

Sass, Tish. "What Others Say", *Writer's Lifeline* (Canada), 1986 No. 5.

Sharma, Jagjit K. "New Books of Poems", *Star India* (Canada), May 14, 1993.

Shukla, Rajesh. "Peace and Understanding", *Christian Monitor* (India), October 2, 1981.

Singh, Pritam. "Little Punjab in Canada", *Advance* (India), June 1990.

Singh, R.K. "Cross-Cultural Communication", *Language Forum* (India), Vol. xxxiv, No. 1-2, Jan-Dec. 1998.

-------- and Sarkar, Mitali De. "A Search For Elysium", *The Mawaheb International* (Canada), June 1998.

Singh, S. "Sketches of India", *Writer's Lifeline* (Canada), July 1982.

Sinha, Bobbie. "Peace and Love", *Byword* (India), June-July, 1992.

Sinha, Ravi Nandan. "Introduction", *Divergent Shades.* Ranchi: Writers' Forum, 1995.

Skogsholm, Gunvor. "Fine Crafted Poetry", *Poetry Forum* (USA), January 1992.

Suprovat Sarkar. "Poems by Stephen Gill", *The Linla* (Canada), Feb. 15 & March 1, 1975.

Tandon, N.K. "Discovery of Bangladesh", The *Canadian India Times*, Dec. 11, 1975.

Tierney, Frank. "Reflection of an Indian Poet", *The Canadian India Times,* Nov. 15, 1973.

Wadlow, Rene V.L. "Anti-War Poems", *Transnational Perspectives* (Switzerland), Vol.13, No. 3, 1987.

Wangu, J.L. "An Interview with a Canadian Author", *The Indian Teacher* (India), Vol. 1, No.2, Jan-Feb., 1979.

Westcott, W.F. "*Immigrant*", *Christian Monitor* (India), November 2, 1980.

Wiles, Clifton A. "The Flowers of Thirst", *al-mohajer* (Canada), No. 4, April 1994.

Wouk, Judith. "Children's Stories: A Comparison", *Writer's Lifeline* (Canada), No. 3, 1986.

Index